Desert Song

Claiming Joy while Walking the Wilderness

BRITTNIE BLACKBURN

WestBow
PRESS®
A DIVISION OF THOMAS NELSON
& ZONDERVAN

Scripture quotations marked NIV are taken from the Holy Bible, New International Version. NIV. Copyright 1973, 1978, 1984 by International Bible Society. Used by permission of Zondervan. All rights reserved.

Scripture quotations marked MSG are taken from The Message. Copyright 1993, 1994, 1995, 1996, 2000, 2001, 2002, 2003 by Eugene H. Peterson. Used by permission of NavPress Publishing Group.

Images from Tiffany Fetter

WestBow Press books may be ordered through booksellers or by contacting:

WestBow Press
A Division of Thomas Nelson & Zondervan
1663 Liberty Drive
Bloomington, IN 47403
www.westbowpress.com
1 (866) 928-1240

ISBN: 978-1-5127-7023-0 (sc)
ISBN: 978-1-5127-7024-7 (hc)
ISBN: 978-1-5127-7022-3 (e)

Library of Congress Control Number: 2016921473

Print information available on the last page.

WestBow Press rev. date: 01/10/2017

Dedication

To my three precious children, who hold my heart every minute of every day.

Clara, you radiate joy each and every day. My days feel light because of your presence. Your life might look different from a typical child your age, but in my eyes, you are perfection.

Camille, you are my spunky, hilarious sidekick. I love, love laughing with you and exploring the world with you. You are a thoughtful sister and daughter.

And to my sweet Chance, you touched my heart and my life and so many others in our five hours together. While you are not with us, your memory lives on. I love you deeply and cannot wait to see you on the other side of time.

Introduction

I sit trembling as I type this introduction. It is a weird feeling to write something no one is asking me to write—or I guess I should say, that no *professional* is asking me to write. To put myself out there and start a project no one is asking me to start. To jump off the deep end when no one is asking me to jump seems a bit strange and, well, crazy.

But when you feel it in the depths of your soul, that undeniable leading, nudging, pointing from the Lord to get your words down on paper, you obey. Well, let's be honest … maybe not immediately. I've been sitting on this project for many, many months now, for goodness' sake. But after more than a year of coincidences and constant tugging and leadings from the Spirit, I can sit no longer. I'm giving in, in Jesus's name and in the confidence that someone out there might gain an ounce of hope from this journey of mine. So here we go.

This is my story of struggle and hope and love and loss and grief and questioning and joy and the miracle of abundant beauty arising from ashes. This is my story of learning how to sing when God asked me to walk through the desert, more than once. This is about how claiming joy is possible even in the midst of our desert places. This is my story of how I have learned (and am still learning) to die to fleshly expectations and embrace the beauty and joy in the circumstances God gives me, not longing for what could have been. This is my joy song birthed from battling trials that only God can win. Trials such as anorexia, infertility, parenting a special-needs child, and birthing a stillborn child. This is my story of praise given new life after countless tears and hands thrown high in the air, calling out to the One who can make all things new. And He did.

Because you see, sometimes God makes it clear that the life you envisioned is not the life to which He has called you. And in this moment of revelation, you get a choice. You can choose to wallow and sulk and become bitter and angry, or you can make room in your heart for *different*—whatever different may be at that moment. If you do the work, really wrestle through the letdowns and emotions and spend time watering any seed of faith you have left, you just might find joy and beauty on the other side. Joy and beauty *even in the middle* of the wandering. Because, sweet friend, joy is available even in the middle of our pain. Joy is not tied to our circumstances. What a sweet blessing and promise from our Father.

This book is a memoir, my personal testimony seasoned with practical reflection (which I refer to as "Real Talk") and action steps for you as the reader. My hope is that by truly taking the time to work through some of these action steps, you will be one step closer to full-out surrender—laying down your hurts, your life, and your expectations at the cross once and for all in exchange for abundant joy. It's not easy—in fact, it is just plain hard—but it's worth it.

I'm sure this won't be the last time God asks me to walk the valley of disappointment or darkness. Yet, ever so softly, He is teaching me a song of praise: *Yes, Lord. I trust you in even this, in this precious journey, this unique calling, this desert place, this life that looks different than I originally expected.*

May it be so for you too.

"But I trust in your unfailing love, my heart rejoices in your salvation. I will sing to the Lord, for he has been good to me" (Psalm 13:5-6).

Contents

Chapter 1

Middle School and Slim Fast Bars

I walked into the gymnasium as a new sixth grade student at my new public school and felt like I could burst. Completely burst. I was surrounded by a sea of middle school students I didn't know. I wanted to run and hide, not be forced to make friends and find my classes after moving to a strange city, something my parents had promoted as "a blessing." I was scared to death.

As an introvert, the thought of navigating my way through unknown halls amidst thousands of strangers made me want to puke and call it a sick day. Or a sick month. That sounded better. Let's not even talk about being forced to race from one end of the building to the other between classes to work a locker that made no sense to my brain. To the self-conscious new girl, working a locker meant *all eyes on me* so I better be quick and not mess up. *Fun* and *exciting* are not words I would use to describe my first week of sixth grade.

Eventually I allowed myself to calm down (a bit) and made one friend, Lisa. She was sweet and shy and super-awkward, just like me. Okay, she was a nerd, just like me. Regardless, I was thankful to have my one nerd friend because, at the end of the day, I had *someone*. Lisa and I had several classes together. We started our day with gym.

Did you get that? First-period gym class. Why schools think it wise to make kids start their school day by getting nasty and stinky and sweaty, I will never know. Walking through the scary halls of middle school is bad enough; let's not add body odor to the situation.

But moving on.

A prerequisite of gym class was changing into our flattering and stylish gym uniforms before gathering together to begin the morning's activities. Do you know how many times I prayed that Hula-Hoop was on the schedule and not soccer or flag football? Please refer to the paragraph above regarding middle school body odor.

It was in this daily changing from school clothes to P.E. uniform that I first remember body image insecurities. We were forced to change in the girls' locker room, and I began to notice that one thing was not like the others. As my eyes wandered around that locker room, I grew anxious about my figure and eventually deemed myself too big. Every day I would make my way to an awkward corner to hide out so that the skinny girls would not see my non-skinny thighs. I opened the door to body image comparison, and little did I know, it would take me nearly fifteen years to shut that door again once and for all.

I somehow survived that first year at my new public school, and I was now at a new private school. Yep, just as I was getting comfortable with Lisa and our fellow nerds, my parents deemed it best we switch from public to private education. I was sad to leave my big, scary school, not because I loved it but because I didn't want to face another change, even if I knew deep down I was better suited for success in a smaller schooling environment. And while I said good-bye to those two thousand students, I did not say good-bye to comparison. The mental games were strong, and I was fully engaged in comparing my body to those who crossed my path. My seventh grade year went well, all things considered, and I even made some non-nerd friends! When summer rolled around, I found it the ideal time to go on my first diet.

I was thirteen years old and convinced I was fat.

Did you catch that?

I was thirteen years old.

On my quest to look like all my skinny—and it was then that I translated *skinny* to mean beautiful—friends, a diet was the natural answer to my dilemma. I made this decision discreetly and decided it would be my little summer resolution. My personal quest to feel good about my body. While all my friends were out living the carefree lives of summer swim parties and sleepovers, I was reading nutrition labels and counting fat grams. I lost thirteen pounds (ironic, no?) and was so proud of my accomplishment. It was that same summer that boys in the youth group started to notice me, and I was added to their "fine girls" ranking list of all the girls at church. I was elated! I was making my way off the nerd list to the acceptable list, and all I had to do was lose weight! A few of the popular boys (what does this even mean?) began talking to me and taking an interest in me and even making a few phone calls to my house to chat every now and then. I cannot even begin to tell you what we talked about, but I'm sure it was riveting because *middle school*. I even remember getting so excited when one of the popular, cute boys asked me to ride go-carts with him at a youth group event.

Go-carts. Such an amazing moment in time.

My adolescent philosophy that skinny equaled beautiful was confirmed. I had the evidence in the eyes of my peers. Chubby Brittnie does not get the same attention as Skinnier Brittnie. I filed that tidbit away as wisdom and continued to fascinate myself with all things food and nutrition.

Fast forward a few years. I was in high school. I was happy, thriving in school, and blessed with a solid group of friends, both at church and at school. While I wasn't fat by any means, I was definitely bigger than most of my girlfriends, my sisters, and my mom. It appeared that all the significant women in my life were shopping for size 2–4 and I was shopping for size 8–10. I had not been able to maintain that middle school summer diet of Special K, but I was starting to think it was worth revisiting.

Satan knew he had a hold of my heart and pressed in hard. He set in on his attack, and instead of fighting back to claim my identity, I fell for his scheming ways. He is a smart one, that Satan. He is evil, but wicked smart. He knows our weak spots. He knows which areas bring us to our knees without much battering.

I traded God's truth for Satan's lies and set out once again to find perfection.

My parents left town for the weekend, and for some reason, it was only my brother and me at home. I don't recall the specific details, but I remember thinking, *This is my chance to reset my life!* I drove myself to the grocery store and bought several boxes of Slim Fast shakes and bars and Lean Cuisine frozen meals. Surely I could take this fine opportunity to limit my diet and lose some weight.

I look back and wonder what the cashier was thinking that day as she saw a high school female falling prey to marketing schemes. I wonder what she was thinking as she scanned not one, not two, but ten boxes of diet food across the belt. Did she think I was buying the items for myself? For a family member? For a friend?

I arrived back home, unloaded the goods, and my brother, taking one look at my purchases, stated, "Gross." Indeed, bro. Indeed. Gross on so many levels. Gross in taste, of course. (I don't care who you are, you cannot tell me that chalky, bland granola bars with a drizzle of chocolate taste like dessert. Just no.) And gross in the sense that I was buying, both with money and thoughts, into the societal message that thin is best. There is no other way. Skinny equals perfection. If I wanted to be beautiful and happy and have boys notice me again, then I needed to find a way to choke down chocolate shakes that tasted like dirty water.

Real Talk: Have you ever been there? Stuck between God's truth and Satan's lies? Take a few minutes to reflect on the details of your own circumstance. What had/has you stuck?

Action Steps: Divide a piece of paper into two columns and write "*Lies*" on the left side and "*Truth*" on the right. Now dig deep. Don't hold back. Write whatever the Lord places in your heart. There is no right or wrong. If we want to get serious about shutting out Satan's voice, we have to get serious about identifying it.

Comparison and Control

Those sixth grade locker room days set my eyes on the path of looking at my own body (thighs and backside specifically), looking at another women's body, and naming my own as less than. Comparison. According to dictionary.com, comparison means "the act of looking at things to see how they are similar or different," and "the act of suggesting that two or more things are similar or in the same category" (2016).

And this is exactly where I was, constantly looking at the bodies all around me, to see if they could be put in the same category. The problem was that nine times out of ten, my body was the outlier. My body was not like my sister's or mom's or best friend's or acquaintance's. My thighs were bigger and my bottom rounder and my face fuller.

Comparison knocked, and I answered. I welcomed her with an open heart and dedicated eyes. I let her dig deep and take root. And we all know when something takes root, it is not easy to dig up. It's never easy. Oh, how this was true for me.

During my high school and college years, I made it a priority to work out. I enjoyed feeling strong and in shape, but there was always an unsettled feeling under the surface. I played basketball my senior year of high school. And by play, I mean I was on the team but had *zero skills*, so I sat the bench most every game, unless our team was ahead by forty points—then my coach would excitedly announce that I was going in for the last *two minutes* of the game! Oh, dear private school and your all-inclusive rules. Still, I enjoyed the exercise—and by exercise, I mean the suicides and laps I had to run during practice as a result of our team losing the night before, which was clearly not my fault … because *two minutes*.

I did not land a spot on my university's basketball team. (No worries, I didn't try out. Can you imagine?) But I continued to make exercise a pivotal part of my day. Whether before class or after, I would head to the gym for uninterrupted time on the elliptical machine. I would leave those workouts feeling good about my fifty minutes on the hamster wheel, but something was still off.

I enjoyed exercising my body, but the root of my enjoyment was out of whack. My drive to exercise was grounded in the desire to be thinner, skinnier, and more beautiful. I wanted more than a clear head and stronger arms and better endurance. I wanted the size 2 jeans. I wanted to be likeable again. I wanted the freedom that would come with a fifteen-pound-lighter frame.

I craved charm and appeal and loveliness, all things Satan had me believe would come if I weighed just a little less.

Comparison was a constant, and thus, a discontented heart was a constant. My eyes were so focused all around me, looking side to side, that I didn't even think to look up. They say that comparison is the thief of joy, but now I know better.

Comparison is the thief of anything and everything good.

When my eyes are busy looking all around me, taking in others' bodies and homes and successes and lives, there is no room left for viewing my own blessings. My lens is tainted. My glasses are scratched, and I always view what I have as not enough. What a sad place to be, dear sister.

I took my wandering eyes and restless heart all the way to Missouri for graduate school. I had started dating my now-husband, Brandon, the last semester of our senior year of college. Since we knew marriage was in the future, he took the leap and moved to the Midwest in the name of love. I was pursuing a master's degree in social work at Washington University in St. Louis and was eager for this new life phase. (Now, before you get impressed with my smarts due to the previously mentioned institution, please just know I had no desire to go to a smart kids' school. My decision-making consisted of researching all the MSW programs that did not require the GRE for acceptance and applying only to those. Somehow Wash U gave me a chance because I can write a mean essay on all things social justice. Just don't sit me down with a timed test, okay? This, said the girl who made a 950 on her SAT. Just sit there for a moment and be amazed.)

School was rough. And by rough, I mean I was trying to manage a full semester of classes while throwing myself into essays and group projects, while feeling out of sorts because the tiny Christian bubble I had lived in the prior four years had been popped. And not just popped—it was sent spinning all the way back to Abilene, Texas. Christianity was not a popular life choice among my new peers, and they were not timid in sharing their logic behind their disapproval. I was inundated with questions and debates (some during class), and for the first time ever in my life, I was forced to defend the reasons behind my faith.

I called my parents several months in, giving them a list of all the reasons this decision to relocate up west was a big fat mistake.

"It's too hard!"

"I don't fit in!"

"These people are relentless!"

"I cannot possibly live here for another year and a half!"

"Maybe this is God's way of telling me I made the wrong choice!"

I hung up the phone angry and confused as my parents *highly encouraged* me to press on and stick it out. *Easy for them to say,* I thought. They were not the ones living this life. They were not the ones stuck in a room for fifty minutes, three times a day, with faith haters.

But I pressed on and continued to give it my all. I threw myself back into workouts as a way to ease stress. It worked. The more time I spent on the treadmill, the more my mind was able to breathe. What began as a three-time-a-week, thirty-minute regime eventually morphed into an everyday, sixty-minute regime.

And for the first time, I noticed something. I was losing weight. I was starting to shed the pounds, and my thighs were looking a little slimmer and my face a little narrower. *Wow!* I thought. *I am finally, for the first time in my life, yielding the results I have always desired! This is great!* I began tweaking my food choices and realized that if I could eat just a little less at each meal, this would also speed up my progress to skinny. I felt as though I had hit the jackpot. I had a win-win. Not only was I relieving the stress of exams and midterms and a grueling schedule, my size 8 jeans were now unwearable.

My classmates began noticing and commenting on my weight loss with, "You look great!" and, "Have you lost weight? You look really good!" Compliments fueled my fire. If they thought I looked great now, then there must have been something wrong with how I looked before. I secretly loved this new attention. I had a new pep in my step. I was slowly becoming the skinny girl of my dreams. The bodies of others that I had envisioned and envied were now mine for the taking. The comparison games that started in middle school were stronger than ever before. The only difference was now, when comparing, I was in the "better" category. I had to keep up the good work.

It was May 2006, I was ten months into my graduate work, and I made a trip home to visit family. I had no idea Brandon was also traveling home to surprise me and pop the question. We became engaged and celebrated with our families.

This same trip home, my mom stopped me by the kitchen counter. "I've noticed you've lost some weight."

"Yes," I replied. "I've just been so stressed with school. I'm dealing with so much. I'm so busy!" All true. Yet I did not disclose how I was growing obsessed with my gym attendance and eating habits. *She doesn't need to know that part*, I rationalized. *I'm in control of this thing! I'm only down ten pounds. I won't let it get out of hand.* She believed me.

At that point, I believed myself.

Juggling a full schedule of classes and working as an intern at a local adoption and foster care agency, I threw myself back into the ever-increasing demands of each day. It seemed that there was little time for anything besides homework, my job, and visits to the gym. I worked out longer and harder. Burning more calories, plus eating way fewer calories, was transforming my body into the body of my comparison dreams. And what started as a casual ten-pound weight loss quickly became fifteen, twenty, and eventually twenty-five.

For the first time in a long time, I was in control. I was succeeding at the one thing that, up until this point, had always ended in failure. It was not hard to hide my obsession around Brandon. He knew from our undergrad days that frequent trips to the gym were not uncommon. He always saw me eat and assumed I was becoming more interested in clean, healthy foods. He saw the pounds come off, but rationalized that the combined stress from finishing school, working, and planning a wedding were taking a toll. It was common for women to lose weight when multitasking and managing so many life areas.

Over the course of a few months, I adopted the "all or nothing" mentality. I had lost the weight and was afraid that if I gave in to even just a bite of bad food, be it chips or dessert or a dinner roll, all my hard work would be undone. I was relentless about tallying every calorie that passed my lips. Documenting daily the calorie counts of what I ate for breakfast, lunch, and dinner, and then subtracting from it the number displayed under "calories burned" on the treadmill was the only way I knew my efforts would not betray me. There were days when this number was in the six hundred range. The illusion of control was hitting me between the eyes.

To control something is "to exercise restraint or direction over; dominate; command; to hold in check; curb; to eliminate or prevent the flourishing or spread of" (Dictionary.com 2016).

Comparison was the focus of my eyes, but control was the focus of my heart.

Real Talk: Has control ever become the focus of your heart? What areas of life have you been trying to control? Be honest.

Action Steps: What are you gaining by holding onto control? What are you losing? Take some time to think through both prompts and journal your answers. If we want to move in a new direction, simply willing it in our thoughts isn't enough. Quiet any distractions and put pen to paper.

Chapter 2

Worship of Self

Despite my love affair with weight loss, I somehow managed to graduate on time with a decent grade point average. I was done! I had set out to master my one huge goal of earning a graduate degree and moved home with not one but two monumental accomplishments to add to my resume: my degree and my thinness.

I was finally the skinny girl. I was skinnier than my sisters, my mom, and most of my friends. I shopped in the coveted areas of my favorite stores and beamed with pride as I stated to the Ann Taylor LOFT employee, "Size 0, please!" The request for a size 0 eventually lead to size 00, which eventually lead to, "I'm sorry, ma'am, but we don't have anything smaller."

Brandon and I were engaged to be married in early 2007, so for a month and a half, between graduation day and our wedding day, I was living back at home. My parents were members of a gym, so it was easy for me to keep tracking my daily stats of calories out versus calories in. I would head out early in the morning and return home ninety minutes later. After a week or so, my mom inquired. Defensive and afraid that she would discover my newest obsession, I lashed out, proclaiming I was perfectly fine and staying healthy and she should get off my back. But deep down, I knew I couldn't keep up my gym attendance if I wanted a peaceful home life. And I needed to keep the peace before I tied the knot. So I said *good-bye* to the treadmill and *hello* to an ever-increasing compulsion of limiting my diet. Fruit, green veggies, and virtually anything calorie dense was acceptable. Starches, sweets, and virtually anything with a high fat count were unacceptable. If my parents were going to question my hours spent at the gym, fine. I didn't need the gym. I could show them. You could take away my treadmill, but you couldn't take away my control. You could curb my output, but you couldn't curb my input.

The wedding came and went, as did the honeymoon, and I threw myself into the demands of my first job post-graduate school. Brandon and I enjoyed starting anew and building our lives together. The newlywed phase was fun and exciting and a chance for me to take my fixation with thinness to an entirely new level.

When man and woman become husband and wife, they vow to remain each other's first love, second to Christ. I stood on that altar that cold February day, pledging my love, but my eyes were not fixated on my groom.

My eyes were fixated on myself.

As the months passed, I wasn't pouring into my marriage as a new bride should. I was pouring into the false god I had created. My heart was hardening, and my love affair with thinness grew at an astronomical rate. Thinness and the quest to be beautiful became my idol. I couldn't see it at the time and rationalized my actions because I was *still eating* and, viewed in that light, it really could be so much worse, right? *There are women far sicklier than me*, I would tell myself. It wasn't that bad. I could stop at any time.

I had created a golden calf and bowed to it morning, noon, and night.

In the beginning chapters of Exodus, we read that the Israelites were being heavily oppressed. Their masters, the Egyptians, were pressing in strong from all sides. Verse thirteen of chapter one states that the Egyptians "worked them ruthlessly". Regardless, fearing the Israelites were growing in strength and numbers, fearing their strength would become too great, Pharaoh demanded that the midwives kill any baby boy born to a Hebrew. The midwives ignored Pharaoh, and as a result, the Hebrews became even more numerous. Pharaoh didn't stop at the midwives' refusal of bloodshed; he then ordered that all Hebrew baby boys be thrown into the Nile (Exodus 1:22).

As the story continues, we are introduced to Moses, a man who, as a baby, was found floating in a basket in the Nile by Pharaoh's daughter. Moses was raised as an Egyptian and, as a result of watching his people be oppressed and tortured as slaves, killed an Egyptian man out of anger (to defend a Hebrew man being beaten) and hid his body in the sand (Exodus 2:12). Pharaoh learned of Moses's actions and threatened to kill him. Moses fled and settled in the land of Midian, where he was eventually taken in by a man named Reuel and given to Reuel's daughter in marriage. But all the while, "the Israelites groaned in their slavery and cried out, and their cry for help because of their slavery went up to God" (Exodus 2:23). God looked upon His people, had pity on them, and called on Moses to set His people free.

You see, not only were Pharaoh and the Egyptians berating the Hebrew people, they were worshiping over eighty major gods and goddesses (First5.org 2016). They had erected for themselves a village of false gods, of false hope, and they couldn't see past their sin. They were covered by such darkness that they couldn't see the light.

They traded in the one true God for a momentary thrill and called it good.

Oh, how I do this too.

Real Talk: Has there ever been a time in your life when you built an idol and justified it as good? Think back over the course of your life. It might help to look back at periods of striving and preoccupation with the world. Did you worship any momentary thrills?

Action Steps: Write down any idols that come to mind, either past or present. Read through Exodus chapters 1–4 and write down any thoughts or reactions. Pray over your list of idols and ask God to help you tear them down, once and for all.

My idol worship was strong, and bad turned to worse as I willingly continued down the path of self-destruction. I never resumed my exercise regimen, but I was religious about counting any and every calorie. Immersing myself in diet and fitness magazines, I would store away tidbits in my brain so that I would never go back to the former Brittnie. The Fat Brittnie. The Ugly Brittnie. Insert any and every negative adjective here. That is how I viewed my former self. But not anymore—I was new and improved.

My weight occupied my brain space every hour of every day. And I mean *every* hour of *every* day. I could be having a nice conversation with a friend about who knows what, and my face played the part but my thoughts were not present. I acted engaged, but I was not engaged. I would eat breakfast, and then for the next several hours, I'd obsess about what I was going to eat for lunch. My stomach would churn with hunger in between meals, but I would not allow myself a snack. No extra calories were permitted—only those consumed at breakfast, lunch, and dinner. If the hunger became too intense, I would allow myself a diet soda in between meals in an attempt to fill myself up until it was time to eat again.

Limiting ourselves in this way gives us a fictitious sense of power. We restrict our food intake or other behaviors, and it makes us feel strong and mighty and almost omnipotent. *Omnipotent* is not a word needed in my personality profile. Omnipotence is reserved for the one true God, our Lord and Savior Jesus Christ. Yet omnipotent is how I felt.

I had created my own little god, and my constant dedication and worship to it made me feel unstoppable.

I was a weight-loss powerhouse. And I was pleased with my new title. Deep down I knew that something needed to change, that something needed to give. My behaviors were sinful, but I didn't care. Oh, how it pains me to admit that now. But it's true. I did not care. I was convicted by the Lord, several times, but I shut out His voice for the voice of my false god.

I was a modern-day Pharaoh.

When we actively walk in disobedience, we are actively deciding to distance ourselves from our Father.

When we disregard His Word and silence His voice for the voice of our idols, it's as if we are saying to our Creator, "I'm going to take a little trip. I might be back soon or it might be a while. I'll come back when I'm ready, but today is not that day. I'll just take a few more steps in this other direction, okay? But don't worry, Lord, I won't go too far. Just a few more steps."

And step after step after step, the space widens, and the gap between my head and my heart grows. Can I tell you something about this gap? This is where Satan flourishes. The gap is his breeding ground. This is the space where Satan lustfully shines his fraudulent goodness and tries to reel us in even more. He specializes in engaging our hearts and convincing us that what he offers is a lot more fun and a lot more life-giving. It might feel that way, dear friends, but the temporary high we get from tapping into Satan's manipulation will eventually come to a screeching halt.

Exodus 6 begins with Moses questioning God about the

assignment given to him. God had asked Moses to stand up to Pharaoh and request that the Hebrew people be freed to worship the Lord, to close the gap and close the door to pagan worship. I find it interesting here that God promises Moses deliverance. God spells out the outcome. While the assignment seems scary and overwhelming, the Lord told Moses directly how it would all go down. And yet Moses still questions God's assignment for him. Moses eventually gussies up the courage to go before Pharaoh and to request the Israelites be allowed to leave Egypt. The chain of events that happens next is just sobering.

Pharaoh's heart is so consumed with his current state of living in sin that he brings pure destruction upon himself, his people, his family, and his land.

My guess is that Pharaoh couldn't see past the moment. Deciding to free the slaves seemed too big and too scary and too risky. Pharaoh was so absorbed with himself that the idea of there being another way of living, a better way, seemed impossible. I imagine he threw in some rationalizations as well. That's exactly where I was too: so preoccupied with my own sin that taking the leap from sin to freedom seemed unfathomable. Silly, even. Why would I willingly give up the reins? Why surrender when I had never felt this in control of my life?

Pharaoh's heart condition led God to action. Pharaoh's "heart was unyielding," and due to his downright refusal, God brought a storm in the form of plagues. Chapters 7–11 of Exodus spell it out.

Water was turned to blood.

Frogs took over the land.

Gnats infested the province.

Flies swarmed and covered everyone and everything.

Livestock was killed off.

Boils festered on the bodies of men and animals.

Hail beat down relentlessly.

Locusts devoured whatever withstood the hail.

Darkness covered the sky, night and day.

Firstborn sons were executed.

It took ten plagues for Pharaoh to free the enslaved Hebrews. It took ten plagues for him to decide that the risk of staying the same weighed greater than the risk of change. It is now so easy for me to look at this story and wonder, *What on earth was Pharaoh thinking? Was he an idiot? A complete blockhead?* I'm pretty sure I would have let Moses do his thing after my shower started spouting human hemoglobin. Just saying.

But y'all, let's just hold up for one quick second. Before I am too quick to judge Pharaoh and his stupidity, I must take a look in the mirror. Just a few short years ago, I was faced with the same predicament—this same choice! God brought people into my life to speak truth, but my heart was unyielding. God brought people into my life to help peel the scales off my eyes, but I decided scales were a better option than change. So while I judge this Egyptian king for his ignorance, I have to pause for a moment.

Just as Pharaoh created for himself a Messiah complex, so had I.

I'll never forget one Wednesday night at church when a sweet woman (an acquaintance at the time, now a friend) came up to me and, out of the blue, told me she was worried about me and the state of my body, how I looked too thin. She asked if I wanted to get together and talk to her about it. *Um, thank you, but no, thank you very much. Move along now, mmmmkay?*

Yet in an effort to play the game lest I be discovered, I agreed to get together the following week. We exchanged numbers and eventually met over a Starbucks latte, for which, in case you were wondering, I memorized the calorie count and strategically worked that number into my day's allotment so I could sip on it semi-anxiety free. She gave me a Christian book from the local bookstore and offered heartfelt encouragement. Her heart was in the right place, and though her words offered some much-needed hope to my stale spirit, I resisted. I resisted for fear of the unknown. The all-or-nothing mindset was paralyzing me in my tracks. My theory was, *If I begin to eat normally, I will lose all control. I won't be able to stop eating and will gain back all the weight I have lost.* Two more lattes, and I said out of obligation, "Thanks so much. I'll let you know if I'd like to get together again!" Then I deleted her cell number from my phone.

My family was concerned (an understatement), as were my friends, but if their concerns were brought to my attention, I laughed them off or quickly changed the subject. I was not ready to give up the worship of self. God needed a more powerful force, something big and mighty and fierce, to get my attention.

I had no idea what was ahead.

Brandon and I had moved from our first apartment to our first home. It was September of 2008, and we were just getting settled into our new space. Physically, I was knee-deep in boxes, but mentally, I was drowning in my anorexia. No formal diagnosis was given at that point, but I knew this was more than innocent, stress-management weight loss. My head spun from all things food and thinness. All. Day. Long.

Abnormal behaviors that felt *normal* included:

- Restricting my food intake to three "meals" per day and no more. Heaven forbid I eat a snack!
- Creating a list of fear foods that under no circumstance could be eaten. If this rule was broken, for any reason, I would make up for it by eating less at the next meal or the next day.
- Eliminating any caloric drinks from my diet (juice, soda, etc.).
- Measuring my portion sizes prior to eating to ensure calorie count.
- Growing anxious when out to eat, scouring the menu for what I deemed the least caloric option, regardless of whether it sounded good.

- Stepping on the scale first thing in the morning, the number displayed causing either pure elation or pure devastation.
- Stepping on the scale first thing in the afternoon, the number displayed causing either pure elation or pure devastation.
- Stepping on the scale first thing in the evening, the number displayed causing either pure elation or pure devastation.
- Obsessing over "healthy living" blogs, magazines, articles, and the like.
- Continually obsessing over food and thinness. There was nothing else I truly spent time thinking about, and it became extremely hard to concentrate on anything else.
- Hiding my food rituals and obsessions from others (or at least *trying to hide*, but most people caught on quite easily).
- Denying my hunger, even when experiencing hunger pangs.
- Talking about food with others continually and/or cooking for others, then refusing to eat what was made.
- Making excuses for not eating ("I'm stuffed!" or "I just ate an hour ago and am so full!").
- Feeling *extreme* guilt when any of the above behaviors/rules were broken.

I never binged and purged or took a diet pill, which some who struggle with anorexia do, so I continued to justify my actions as not being bad enough to stop. *It could be so much worse! I could be vomiting or gorging on pills, and I'm not!* Even with the laundry list of abnormal behaviors, I made justifications. But how does one justify weighing so little that the seat belt indicator light constantly flashes, not recognizing a body in the driver's seat?

I'll never forget the moment I excused myself to the bathroom one Sunday while eating in another couple's home. I saw a scale in the corner and eagerly took the opportunity for another chance to check in. I stripped off my shoes and my jeans and my shirt to get an accurate number. The number read ninety-two. Ninety-two pounds. Not only was I willing to engage in these ritualistic behaviors at home, they were now transpiring in the homes of others. Vomiting or no vomiting, pills or no pills, this confirmed that my rationale was sinking me deeper and deeper in the quicksand.

<u>Real Talk</u>: What justifications are you making in your life? In what area(s) of your life are you saying to God, "It's not so bad. I could be doing X, Y, or Z, and I'm not! It could be so much worse!"

<u>Action Steps:</u> Write down whatever justifications you are making. Don't just think them; write them. Now pray over this list, one by one, and ask the Father to help break down the walls of pride or entitlement or control. Take it a step further and reveal this list to a friend and ask for prayers. Ask too how you can pray for her. Accountability is a powerful tool in banishing our sin and justifications of it.

Chapter 3

The Plague of Ike

I t was hurricane season, and the city of Houston was prepping for the possibility of storms. Employees all over the Greater Houston area were sent home from work to prepare for Hurricane Ike, a doozy of a storm that was expected to make landfall on Galveston Island on September 13, 2008. Brandon and I came home to *hunker down*, a term I view as comical since it's used by Houstonians in any type of weather threat. The slightest chance of sleet: "*Hunker down, Houston!*" Picture the entire population of Houston swarming Kroger and H.E.B to buy every last bottle of water, candle, flashlight, gallon of milk, and loaf of bread. That's hunkering down, Houston-style.

Brandon's parents came to stay with us for the night since their home was more in the storm's direct path than ours. We were home, our house was attended to, and all there was left to do was sit around and wait.

Day turned to night, and we soon realized that the predictions of fierce wind and rain were right on. I decided to go sleep in our master bedroom, but after an hour, Brandon and his dad made me come join them in the living room where I would be most protected from shattered glass. I was initially annoyed. *You are waking me up from my sweet slumber, asking me to follow you to a safer shelter? Okay, fine. I will, but I won't do it happily.*

I couldn't see it then, but now I recognize the foreshadowing. This is exactly what God was nudging me to do.

Wake up!

You are in danger!

I have a better way!

A safer option!

Give up your will, your attitude, your desires, and follow me to safety!

Quick! Before it is too late!

The four of us, along with my in-laws' cocker spaniel, gathered in our living room, listening to the radio for storm updates. The night crept slowly, hour by hour by hour. It felt like the longest night of my life. As we sat listening to the storm rage outside, my own storm continued to rage on the inside.

According to weather.gov, "Over the warm waters of the Gulf of Mexico, Ike grew in size and intensified to a Category Two hurricane with maximum winds of 100 mph by that evening. Ike continued to move northwest toward the Texas coast as the hurricane crossed the central and northwest Gulf of Mexico. Although Ike's intensity remained in the Category Two range, the cyclone continued to grow and became a very large hurricane. The diameter of tropical storm force winds covered a total of 425 miles from the northwest to southeast as Ike approached the upper Texas coast on Friday, September 12. Ike made landfall at 2:10 a.m. CDT Saturday, September 13, near Galveston, Texas. Ike was a Category Two hurricane at landfall with maximum sustained winds of 110 mph" (2016).

Wind raged outside my door at 110 mph, and all I could think about was what I was going to eat the next day.

We made it through the night with no shattered windows. No one slept but an hour or two, but on the inside, we were safe and protected and seemingly peaceful. Yet, that next morning when we opened the front door for the first time, the truth was revealed. Trees down. Fences broken. Yards in disarray. Homes dismantled. War had been waged, and it would soon be time to rebuild.

Not only had the truth been revealed about the state of our property, it would soon be revealed about the state of my heart. While Brandon and his parents were outside surveying the land and walking the streets and talking to gathered neighbors, I was surveying the number on the scale.

We had just been through a hurricane, and all I wanted to do was rip my clothes off and weigh myself.

I closed myself in our master bathroom, stripped off my pajamas, and stepped on the scale, just like I had done every morning for the last goodness-who-knows how many mornings. And for the first time ever in my quest to thinness, the number flashing under my feet sent shivers down my spine.

Eighty-nine pounds.

I stood there in disbelief. I didn't know what to do. This was the lowest number I had ever seen, and I was scared. Tears welled in my eyes. *What am I doing? Am I really in control? What if I can't stop? What is happening to me?* I was terrified of the reality of these answers. Panic entered my body, but I didn't know what to do with it. Sitting on the cold, tile floor, I wept. I was fearful for my life and the possibility of death.

As the day pressed on, my sadness turned to anger. I knew something in me needed to change lest I die, but I did not want to change. Nothing in me wanted to change. I still desired thinness. Facing my struggle implied that I needed transformation, and not one part of me wanted to transform. Control was something I was not ready to hand over. God had used a natural disaster to wake me from my slumber, but I was not ready to fully wake. So what in the world was I to do?

Real Talk: What internal storm are you facing today? Do you feel God nudging you to arise and awaken from your slumber? Are you ready to hand over control or are you still holding on tight? What scares you about letting go?

Action Steps: Take a few moments to review all the Real Talk prompts up to this point. Write down the themes you see, if any. Name your storm for what it is and lift it up to God. If you are ready to hand over the reins, ask him to take over full control. If you are not quite there, that is okay—ask Him instead to gently guide and open your heart to get you to a place of sweet surrender.

"During the night Pharaoh summoned Moses and Aaron and said, 'Up! Leave my people, you and the Israelites! Go, worship the Lord, as you have requested. Take your flocks and herds, as you have said, and go!' … The Egyptians urged the people to hurry and leave the country. 'For otherwise,' they said 'we will all die!'" (Exodus 12:31–33).

For otherwise, we will all die.

Death was now a risk. Pharaoh had hit his breaking point. He realized the risk of staying stuck was greater than the risk of change, of letting go.

We read through these scriptures and deem him an idiot, but honestly, I empathize with this man. Because I've been in that very spot. I too have been glued in that space where letting go looked really, really scary, and I questioned, "Is it worth it?"

The thought of blood and frogs and flies and boils and even death seems scary, of course, but there is something about taking that first step into freedom, into the letting go, into the unknown, that keeps us cycling back into our sin and hang-ups. Pressing into potential freedom doesn't seem like a gamble worth taking.

Maybe that's where you are today, sweet sister: faltering between whatever perceived safety net you've created and the only safe spot we know to be true—our Lord Jesus.

I imagine God, though stern in His judgment, understood Pharaoh's predicament. And I imagine He understands our predicament today. God, while He desires us deeply, will not force us. We must decide for ourselves that the risk of trading in self-worship for God worship is worth it. We must firmly decide that we want the Lord and we desire to see the beauty and joy in how He created us.

Why is that so hard to do? Because self-worship seems alluring, possibly a little edgy, and worth the pursuit. It is through the idolatry of self that God exposes our hidden expectations. We expect our bodies to look a certain way and our backsides to fit into a certain tag number, and when that tag number is not reality, we take back the reins because surely we know better than the Creator of the universe. Surely, He meant for me to always and forever shop in the juniors section. Surely, He got confused and crafted my hips a little wider and my wrinkles a little deeper. Surely, He just made a little boo-boo thirty-four years ago.

"But who are you, O man, to talk back to God? Shall what is formed say to him who formed it, 'Why did you make me like this?' Does not the potter have the right to make out of the same lump of clay some pottery for noble purposes and some for common use?" (Romans 9:20–21).

I am convicted by these lines in Romans. When we refuse to accept our bodies for what they are, we are essentially sassing back to our Father. We are back-talking the One who spoke the world into existence! If we believe His plans are perfect and His ways are perfect, then why would we shame our bodies to be anything less than perfect?

The One with the paintbrush doesn't make mistakes.

Let that sink in and read it again.

The One with the paintbrush doesn't make mistakes.

If we know that to be true, then we can boldly claim that we walk this world blemish-free! We don't need society's airbrushing and Photoshopping and quick-fix dieting schemes. We need contentment and a free, joy-filled spirit.

You are not a mistake.

Your body is not a mistake.

You hold so much beauty, just the way you are.

Joy is waiting for you on the other side of letting go.

Sisters, it's time to daringly claim this truth in Jesus's name.

Chapter 4

Anorexia's Schemes

An eating disorder is sneaky. Usually no one sees it coming. It nags at you slowly, and at the beginning, you are not aware of its existence. Anorexia starts out small and hints at you in microscopic ways. Then, over time, it begins to grow and fester and linger around, all the while growing more.

This was my experience. What started out as harmless stress control grew to a full-blown obsession of self. Ironically, the more this obsession grows, the more control it makes you think that you have. See the appeal there? We all like the idea of a little more control, right? Since you think you are in the driver's seat, you assume you can dig out its nasty roots at any time. Oh, if only it were this easy.

A friend once asked me, if my eating disorder were a character in the Bible, what role would fit the bill? And my mind quickly landed on the serpent in the Garden. In Genesis 3:1–7, we read that Satan disguised himself as a serpent to slowly and sweetly manipulate Eve into eating that forbidden apple (most likely a pricey Honeycrisp because we can all agree these are the most appealing and delicious apples in the history of apples). That serpent and the beginning stages of an eating disorder have a lot in common. Let's take a closer look.

> Now *the serpent was more crafty than any of the wild animals* the Lord God had made. He said to the woman, *"Did God really say, You must not eat from any tree in the garden?"* The woman said to the serpent. "We may eat fruit from the trees in the garden, but God did say, 'You must not eat fruit from the tree that is in the middle of the garden, and you must not touch it, or you will die.'" *"You will not surely die," the serpent said* to the woman. *"For God knows that when you eat of it your eyes will be opened, and you will be like God, knowing good and evil."* When the woman saw that the fruit of the tree was good for food and pleasing to the eye, and also desirable for gaining wisdom, she took some and ate it. Then the eyes of both of them were opened, and they realized they were naked." (Genesis 3:1–7, emphasis added)

Satan was feeding Eve lies, and she was eating them up. In the same way, Satan was feeding me lies, and I kept biting off more of his lustful apple in an attempt to be like God—to gain ultimate control of my life. If we take a moment to reflect, we can pull three main points in comparing Satan's temping of Eve in the Garden to his tempting of us today.

Manipulation and lies

Perpetrators use manipulation and lies to gain trust with their victims. In the garden, Satan used manipulation to convince Eve that if she just took one bite of the apple, she would be like God and her eyes would be opened to greatness.

In the same way, anorexia lies by telling you that after one restriction you can, and will, walk away like it never happened. For anyone who has struggled with an eating disorder, a common thought pattern is, *Once isn't so bad. Losing five more pounds isn't a big deal. I won't do this for long.* Yet walking away from our weakness is never as easy as we think. It sure wasn't easy for Eve, and it sure wasn't easy for me at the beginning stages of my illness.

Rationalization of poor decisions

I wonder what Eve was thinking the second before she took a bite of the forbidden fruit. I have no idea what was running through her mind, but there had to be some type of rationalization going on in her brain. She rationalized enough to take that first bite and then pass the apple on to Adam. Satan helped Eve justify her decision. So it is at the beginning stages of an eating disorder. Rationalization after rationalization after rationalization. And with each small justification and poor decision, I kept losing myself.

A false sense of confidence

Otherwise known as the "rush factor," anorexia has a way of giving off a rush of feel-good endorphins. The first time you restrict, the first time you see the scale drop, the first time you turn down that dessert when everyone else is eating it, your endorphin levels skyrocket, and you feel that thrill of excitement, confidence, and power.

I remember feeling the rush factor when people started to notice I had lost some weight. This was early on before my anorexia was in full swing. As people commented on my new figure, it made me feel powerful and boosted a false sense of confidence. My guess is that Eve felt that same rush as she bit into that delicious apple.

Looking back on my two years of illness, there are so many things I didn't see right away. Hindsight is, in fact, 20/20. Too bad current sight isn't 20/20 as well because that would make things a whole lot easier on humankind. Nonetheless, since anorexia is sneaky and specializes in deception, it is important to call out its lies for what they are as soon as we recognize them.

When anorexia was tempting me, it didn't disclose all that it would remove from my life. Most addictions don't. Anorexia only illuminated what I might gain. Such is the work of Satan in our lives. Remember, He comes *only* to steal, kill, and destroy (John 10:10). Destruction is his mission.

Satan shines the perceived dreamy and hides the possible dreadful.

What my anorexia didn't tell me:

- I will steal your joy.
- I will never be enough for you.
- I will make you selfish.
- I will play whatever games it takes for you to trust me, but I don't really care about you.
- I will pull you away from your family and friends.
- I will discourage you from participating in social events.
- I will create a defensive nature within you.
- I will harden your heart.
- I will steal your peace.
- I will consume your thoughts.
- I will feed your soul with lies.
- I will inhibit your ability to love.
- I will make you feel that God has abandoned you.
- I will never tell you how beautiful you are.
- I will become your obsession.
- I will never fill your soul the way Jesus can.
- I will bring a spirit of condemnation.
- I will instill an immense sense of guilt within you, and this guilt will keep you from asking your family, friends, God, and/or professionals for help.
- I will fill your heart with shame.
- I will make your hair lose its shine, bounce, and luster, and it will fall out.

- I will make your nails paper thin.
- I will make you cold, despite the actual temperature.
- I will completely zap your energy.
- I will change your skin from soft to sandpaper.
- I will make you grumpy, all day, every day.
- I will disrupt your sleep.
- I will slow down your metabolism.
- I will shut down your body's natural processes, in more ways than one.
- I will inhibit your ability to conceive a child naturally.

Can we park here for just a second? Reread the list above and let it sink in deep. This list is the perfect picture of our enemy, who fools us into believing a life with him is better than a life with Jesus. The enemy specializes in nondisclosure! He draws us in with the pros but doesn't expose the cons. This type of opponent spends day and night plotting against you and me. Satan is real and alive, and his daily to-do list revolves around our ruin.

> [The locusts] invaded all Egypt and settled down in every area of the country in great numbers. Never before had there been such a plague of locusts ... They covered all the ground until it was black. They devoured all that was left after the hail—everything growing in the fields and the fruit on the trees. Nothing green remained on tree or plant in all the land of Egypt. (Exodus 10:14–15)

Just as the locusts consumed the land and overtook every space of Egypt, so had my anorexia taken over every space of my life. My ground was black. My life was devoured by my own self-destruction. I had nothing left to offer, nothing left to give. There was no room for depth and growth in the life I was living.

I wasn't really living. I was lifeless.

Real Talk: Read over the list above one more time. Does this list tug at your heart in any way? In what ways is Satan shining the dreamy and hiding the dreadful in your own life? Food might not be your struggle, but is there another stronghold that needs attention?

Action Steps: Make your own list. Name everything Satan is stealing from you as you entertain his lies. Be completely honest with this list. This action step might take a bit more time than the previous exercises. That is okay. Spend as much time as you need, maybe even a day or two. Reflection and honest action is how we break into sin areas that need mending.

I finally decided the risk of staying the same was greater than the risk of change. The locusts had eaten thirty pounds of me, and I was scared of what would happen if I kept letting them run loose. I wanted to be a mother someday, and since menstruation had ceased, I was not only jeopardizing this dream for myself, but I was also threatening Brandon's dream of becoming a father. And that just plain wasn't fair. The thought that my selfishness could impede our future with children was enough to point my feet toward my first *big* baby step. While it was an itty-bitty step in the grand scheme of recovery, it was monumental in my head and in my heart.

I admitted to Brandon I needed help. We talked, I cried, and he supported me. I also called my mom to let her know I was sick and ready for change. We talked, I cried, and she supported me. I asked that she inform my dad and siblings too. This was such a leap of faith in a new direction, and I just didn't have it in me to face up to anyone else in that moment. Looking back now, I'm so thankful for my family's love and grace. They helped encourage and push me forward instead of dwelling on all my mistakes from those two (but felt like ten) years. They saw me as beautiful, just as God did, and still does, regardless of what the scale read or the tape measured.

Do you believe that for yourself? Do you believe that you are beautiful, flawless in His eyes—sunspots, wrinkles, mommy pooch, and all? Please hear me: We are not talking about perfection. We are not talking about never sinning and always loving and never losing your marbles because, oh my goodness, it's 5:00 p.m. right now and I think my kids are *losing their sweet minds*. No, dear friends. The only perfect being that ever walked this earth was Jesus, and we are not expected or required to live up to His model.

Imperfection and flawlessness can coexist. We can claim imperfection while still claiming flawless identity in Christ.

The only way I have come to live in this truth is to throw my expectations into the fire. Lay 'em down, and burn 'em up. We lay down our expectations of perfection, and pick up the beauty and one true joy that comes with a flawless identity in our only reliable life source, Christ. He gifted us this identity on the cross, sisters. No one can snatch that from our hands, and neither can a pair of size 00 skinny jeans. If we don't lay down our expectations of what our bodies should be, our hands will be too full for anything else. Our hands will be too full for the good stuff! What a sad reality! God is sitting up there with all these blessings ready to be claimed, but we have no time to claim them because we are physically starving our bodies and daydreaming about all the food we wish we could eat.

Chapter 5

Hunger Pangs

There I was, stuck between not wanting to give up control and knowing I needed to. I decided my next big baby step would be hiring a nutritionist to evaluate my current diet and help me gain back the needed weight. I could have done this on my own. I was smart enough nutrition-wise and knew the types of healthy foods to eat and everyday changes to make to put the pounds back on, but I needed the accountability. I needed someone outside of myself, with no emotional ties, to meet with me weekly and keep me on track. If I left it up to myself, I would have caved. If I left it up to a family member or a friend, I would have fired them after the first meeting.

I assumed I didn't need a therapist because all I needed to do was gain back the weight. (You can go ahead and take a second to laugh at that assumption.) But, joking aside, I did not think there was any mental health work needed. I was too skinny, and all of my strongholds would be removed once I was back to a typical weight. It was just that simple. While Brandon didn't agree with this logic, he knew this road to recovery was a marathon and not a sprint, and mile marker number one was getting me into the office of that nutritionist.

I called to set up my first appointment, and Dr. R asked that I write down everything I ate for the few days that lead up to the visit so that she could get a clear baseline of what we were working with.

I walked in that first day, and in my little notebook read the following:

Breakfast: Two instant oatmeal packets made with water, coffee with sugar-free creamer

Lunch: Turkey sandwich on 40-calorie bread with mustard, 60-calorie pudding cup

Dinner: Rice and veggies with a little bit of chicken

Dessert: Diet hot chocolate made with water

I am sure Dr. R was gagging at the thought of choking down 40-calorie, no-taste bread and 25-calorie hot chocolate *mixed with water*. Let's unpack this for a quick second. I don't know what qualifies as dessert in your mind, but please, just say no to the diet hot chocolate. This nightly beverage, which I looked forward to every single day, tasted like water with an extra scoop of dirt. There is not enough money in the world to get me to drink that junk again.

Dessert is meant to be luscious and deliciously rich. *This drink is not that at all.* I passed on so many good dessert options those two years, and I don't get that time back. I am making up for it now, though—don't you worry. I'm looking at you, Ben and Jerry's Chocolate Therapy (no pun intended).

Dr. R would weigh me at the beginning of every visit, track my progress, and then review my food journal from the previous week to see where I could make little changes that might make a big difference calorie-wise, but wouldn't feel like I was adding much more food to my diet. Rule 101 of recovery: If you want to stick with a healthy meal plan, make tiny changes that make a big impact. Someone with an eating disorder will not automatically add fear foods or an extra meal to the day's diet. She challenged me, week after week after week, to tweak my meal plan in various ways. Here are a few examples:

- Drinking 1 cup of juice with my breakfast
- Adding 1 tablespoon of peanut butter to my morning oatmeal, or when eating cereal, using 2 percent milk in place of skim
- Drinking a Boost or similar protein drink as a midmorning snack
- Adding 2 tablespoons of mayo and one slice of cheese to my turkey sandwich
- Replacing my pudding cup with a yogurt *(healthier and higher in calories and protein)*
- Adding 10-20 almonds as an afternoon snack *(lots of bang for your buck here)*
- Adding olive oil to my veggies/chicken and cheese to my rice at dinner *(She also suggested avocado slices, which is a perfect option when looking for a nutritious food packed with good calories and healthy fats, yet due to a food sensitivity, that was not an option.)*
- Using milk in place of water for my nightly hot chocolate

I wish I could say that I set out with my new and improved meal plan and never looked back. But it wasn't that easy. I incorporated some of her suggestions but not all of them. One of the hardest parts of those beginning days of recovery, for me, was that I battled whatever food rules I created. I was forcing myself to step outside my comfortable box and into the land of the unknown. I was in bondage and craved freedom, but I knew in order to get there, combat would be necessary. Head-to-head and sword-to-sword, I was in battle. I had to fight, and fight well, with whatever strength I could muster.

Some food rules I battled in those early days included consuming liquid calories, eating between meals, incorporating fear foods (pizza, chips, bread, dessert of any kind), and growing comfortable with the feeling of fullness.

I was so used to the feeling of hunger that the concept of fullness petrified me.

I knew what the pangs of hunger meant. Hunger pangs implied that I was still in control, I was in charge, and I was winning. Surrendering to this hunger was like stepping into the abyss of the scary and unknown. Questions loomed. *Will I automatically get fat? Will I be able to stop eating? What if I lose all control? What happens then? Will people think of me as a fake?*

If my body was a well, I was dried up, with no fresh water in sight. Replenishing this dry well feels unnerving at first. It feels wrong. Have you been there too? Giving into our hunger pangs doesn't only apply to food. Hunger pangs, those deep places of our lives that need filling, can be a number of things: marital stress, stubbornness, pride, deceitfulness, gossip, financial stress, a health diagnosis, or _____ (you fill in the blank). All these areas of hunger need filling. We must go to battle for this fullness. Lasting fullness only comes from facing our fears head-on and battling them down to the ground. But here's the cool part:

You are never *required to fight alone.*

We have the Spirit of the Living God available to us at any moment of any day. We have His power ready for the taking, ready for battle; but we have to tap into it in order for it to activate. When we are weak, He is our strength. When we can't face another day succumbing to our strongholds, He is our strength. When we cannot see beyond the moment of despair, He is our strength. And He wants us to *win* this fight, friends. Remember, you are never required to fight alone.

> Moses answered the people, "Do not be afraid. Stand firm and you will see the deliverance the Lord will bring you today. The Egyptians you see today

you will never see again. The Lord will fight for you,
you need only to be still" (Exodus 14:13–14).

Do not be afraid.

Stand firm.

Deliverance will be yours *today*.

Your stronghold, whatever is enslaving you, will be
knocked down.

The Lord will fight for *you*.

Just be still.

And then get ready to claim the joy that comes from
sweet victory.

I set out with the goal of trading in skim milk for the blasted
2 percent. I was not happy about this in the slightest, but I knew I
had to do it. I typically grocery shopped alone and at my leisure on
those days (um, with no kids, grocery shopping during those years
was basically a vacation!), but I needed Brandon for this trip. We
worked our way through the produce section and circled around to
the dairy department. I got to the door that held the milk *I didn't
want to buy* and froze. I just stood there, unable to open the door.
Brandon put his hand on my back and said, "You need to be the one
to get that milk. You can do it. Take as much time as you need."

Bless him. He knew this was something I had to do on my own.
Could he have easily opened the door, grabbed the 2 percent, thrown
it in the cart, and called it a day? Yes, of course. But he knew, as
did I, that this was a choice I had to make. No one else could make

it for me. I was the one in battle, and I had to take that first step toward a better life.

Tears came. I just stood there with sadness and anger and a sense of betrayal to my beloved skim, but with a slight glimmer of hope for a life richer and more full of joy than the one I was living. It took me twenty minutes to retrieve that 2 percent. Twenty minutes. But I did it, in Jesus's name and with Jesus's help. "If you want me to buy this stupid milk, you're going to have to *show up*," is what I kept telling God in that very moment.

Let's just pause for a quick second. Are you getting this full picture? Crazy, emotional girl standing in front of the milk section, crying her eyes out, unable to move, and bargaining out loud with God? Well, that's special. My fellow shoppers didn't know what they were getting themselves into that day. Kroger down the street, I sincerely apologize if your sales dropped after that amazing theatrical event. Actually, now that I think about it, that Kroger later went out of business.

Real Talk: What hunger pangs need addressing? Today, what is gnawing at the pit of your stomach that needs deep nourishment?

Action Steps: Write down one step, one way, that you will go to battle to fill your hunger. Be realistic. Don't bite off more than you can chew in this moment. You don't need to list fifteen steps—just one. Now, take what you have written and post it around your house, in your car, or in your Bible for inspiration. Lastly, pray that God will activate strength within you to see it through.

God does not expect us to live in the desert alone with our hunger. He is the way to fresh water!

But He requires some action on our part. He expects us to do some hard work and heavy lifting. If you feel stuck in that place where I was, between knowing you need to let go but not wanting to let go, please trust me when I encourage you to take that one baby step you listed above and give it a try. Take action. We will never accept our flawless identity in Christ until we close our eyes and surrender to that first thing. Just see what happens. What do you have to lose?

Dr. R continued to scrutinize me weekly (she was quite kind, but I felt like I was in the hot seat). She was so patient and loving. But as I mentioned before, I just couldn't do some things she suggested. And that is okay. The key is that I was doing something toward my goal of a healthier me. Something is better than nothing. The daily Boost between breakfast and lunch? I only did that once and, for whatever reason, it was too hard. I told her I would eat two slices of cheese on my sandwich instead of drink that horrid brown liquid. She agreed. To this day, I can't pass the nutritional drink aisle of the grocery store without thinking of sweet Dr. R.

The pounds started to come on, but I felt a little unsettled. I (still) was not happy about having to gain the weight. I knew if I wanted lasting change, I needed a full heart makeover, not just a Band-Aid. Gaining weight was a great start and set my feet on the right path, but I needed deeper intervention to prevent relapse. I made the decision to hire a therapist.

"Real freedom won't occur with just an external relocation. It requires a complete internal renovation." (First5.org. 2016)

I got a referral from my sweet friend whose phone number I had deleted from my cell phone months prior. (Remember her? The woman who called me out at church? She never gave up on me.) And I set up my first appointment with Dr. J.

This is where I break regularly scheduled programming to promote all things therapy. Y'all, do it. I don't care if you don't think you have any issues to work out because your life is all roses and tulips. I promise you will walk away feeling lighter. These people get paid to help us feel better and live better! Tap into this resource! When I have a friend who is contemplating therapy but on the fence due to a certain stigma, this is what I say: "Girl, if my money grew on the trees in my backyard, I would go to therapy *every single day of my life*." If anything, it is one hour where you can sit on a comfy couch and sip your Frappuccino and let the words flow and not be interrupted, spit up on, or pooped on by small humans. I'm serious. Don't delay. Set up your therapy appointment today!

Therapy visits can be awkward at first, but that feeling soon dissipates. That said, this initial awkwardness is different from not meshing well with your counselor, so if weeks go by and you just aren't feeling it, cease visits and hire someone else. Be careful not to confuse "not meshing well" with "I don't want to do what they are telling me to do because it's hard." Therapy is hard work. If it wasn't hard, we wouldn't need these people to begin with. Push past the initial weirdness, but continue your search if you feel in your gut something is off.

I started seeing Dr. J twice a week at first. Slowly, as progress was made, we reduced sessions to once a week, and eventually from twice a month to once a month. It is commonly said, and very true, that eating disorders are rarely ever about the food. This was true for me. Yes, I loved feeling and being skinny, but feeling and being skinny was just the top layer of a gigantic Jenga puzzle. Whether we are eating too much or not enough, food, at its core, is not the problem. Food is the tool used to manipulate and the weapon we throw at deep-seated issues.

If we want lasting change, we have to dig up the roots to create space for new life. Joy emerges as we dig up our junk. I did my fair share of digging over three years with Dr. J and faced, head-on, issues such as insecurity, comparison, control, self-worship, and people pleasing. I had to tend to each of these areas to make the way for the best way: God's way.

I read a daily online devotional by Proverbs 31 Ministries, and a commenter once stated: "When we are looking for something apart from God to quell unrest or offer encouragement, we are choosing idolatry over Jesus."

God created us not just to live but to thrive; but we can't thrive if our heads are hung low and our eyes are looking at everyone but Him. Peel your eyes away from the woman next door and look up. You were both created uniquely and perfectly in His image. Both of you! He didn't create her without flaws and give them all to you. He didn't create her and deem His creation good and create you and deem His creation less than. That is not how He works. Let Him prune you so that He can fill you. Let Him be enough.

Real Talk: Do you feel empty, like there is a deep, dark hole in your heart that needs filling? Food, or lack thereof, will never fill this hole, sweet sister. It was never intended to. Only God can fill that space. Or if not food, what have you been stuffing in the hole of your heart instead of letting God in?

Action Step: Say this prayer: *Dear Father, I confess that I have been avoiding you and using other means to fill the spaces of my life that only you can fill. God, give me strength to take a step of faith today. Give me a mustard seed of faith to make a different choice today. Lead me into a new way of living today. Your Word tells us that you are loving and faithful and true. If you are for me, who can be against me? No one, Father. Help me when I feel weak and want to crawl back to my former habits. Break me to build me. In Jesus's name, Amen.*

Chapter 6

Deliverance

You might be thinking, *Okay, I get the point. But how do I actually get there? How do I start laying down these bodily hang-ups I have created to embrace the true beauty in the body I have actually been given?*

I have walked in your shoes. There were so many days I cried buckets of tears, wailing, "This is too hard. I just can't do this anymore!" There is no quick fix or three-step program. Oh, how I wish there were. But change happens over time, little by little, if you are willing to put in some hard work. Sometimes being obedient to God just looks like plain hard work, no? If change were easy, then we probably wouldn't appreciate how far He has brought us in our journey. If change were easy, we would miss the joy in His faithfulness. We probably wouldn't appreciate the freedom from our enslavement and the manna He sends straight from heaven along the way.

"And on that very day the Lord brought the Israelites out of Egypt by their divisions" (Exodus 12:51).

Can you imagine? Finally! After all the blood, sweat, and tears, Moses and the Israelites were set free, once and for all. Deliverance had come. It was theirs for the taking. This doesn't mean the rest of their journey felt easy. They still had to face the enemy and trust God to part the waters of the Red Sea, but through trust and obedience, "the Israelites went through the sea on dry ground, with a wall of water on their right and on their left. That day the Lord saved Israel from the hands of the Egyptians, and Israel saw the Egyptians lying dead on the shore" (Exodus 14:29–31).

Like He did for Israel, God wants to part the waters for us and longs for our idols to be left for dead on the shore. He wants us embracing our true selves, as He created us. He wants joy to flourish!

Here are a few practical points of application that helped me let go of expectation and embrace the beauty in the real me, in the real body gifted to me by my perfect Creator. Some of these suggestions might seem childlike, but I promise you, the resulting freedom is worth it. The ideas below can be applied to any area of life that needs attention.

Name Your Idol

When my therapist first suggested this exercise, I wanted to laugh in her face. Give my anorexia a name? Isn't that, like, *a little weird?* Yet, I had nothing to lose, so I went for it. Instead of giving the disease a traditional name like *Rachel* or *Sarah*, I just named it *E.D.*, short for eating disorder. The goal in naming our idols is that anytime we struggle mentally, we can stop and say quite firmly, "This is E.D. talking to me right now, and she is not my friend." Or "E.D., I am not listening to you any longer." Or "E.D., you are not worth my time." Insert a thousand and one examples here, but you get the idea. It is also important to speak out loud, not just in your head.

There is power when you physically hear your voice. Hearing your voice prompts you into action more quickly than if you just rely on the script in your head. I will say I got a few *really strange looks* that day in Kroger when I had that conversation with myself over purchasing the 2 percent milk. But hey, the point is I walked away that day with the 2 percent. Take that, E.D.

Create Some Visuals

If we are going to replace mental mind games with freedom and reclaim our joy, we need some solid visual aids. Visual reminders keep us on track by pointing us to truth when our minds (and Satan) attempt to lure us in the wrong direction. Here are a few ideas for creating your own visuals.

- Write out key scriptures on sticky notes and tape them around your house, your car, or your office. If you are overwhelmed and don't know where to start, try looking up one or all of these verses: Psalm 139:14, 1 Corinthians 6:19–20, Philippians 1:6, Philippians 4:19, Isaiah 58:8, Joshua 1:9.
- Take a Sharpie to your scale and write, "You are more than a number!" I did this, and any time I walked into the bathroom, I had a reminder of truth in my face. Seeing this phrase also steered me away from unnecessary weight check-ins. Remember, that number is just that: a number. It is part of you but not the whole of you.
- Create a set of recovery cards. Recovery cards are cards (or it can be anything that works for you) where you list out *all* of the positive benefits of choosing change over staying stuck. For more details, see the section below titled List the Benefits of Change.

Trash Any Visuals that Are Holding You Back

Go through your mail and your e-mail, and look at who you are following on social media. Do these outlets, these people, speak God's truth? Or do they intensify comparison, control, and idolatry? Unsubscribe and unfollow any outlet that is causing you to stay stuck in unhealthy habits and unhealthy thoughts. "Ten foods to blast belly fat?" Delete. "Three days to a slimmer, more beautiful you?" Trash. That celebrity you think is fun, but who constantly posts photos of her half-naked self? Unfollow. If we want to take steps in a new direction, we have to relentlessly rid ourselves of the media's standard of beautiful.

Friends, we were never meant to be Barbie. Did you know that if Barbie were a real woman, she would most likely have to walk on all fours due to body disproportionality? Barbie is an unrealistic fictional character, as are most other in-your-face media messages. God created you as a very real character in this life. Be relentless. Trash the trash.

List the Benefits of Change

During one of my earliest therapy sessions, Dr. J challenged me create a list of both physical and psychological benefits of my life without anorexia. She asked that I bring these to her at our next session. I did, and from then on, I carried these recovery cards with me everywhere and (eventually) taped both lists to my bathroom mirror where I would see them every day.

It is so important to have a clear vision of what you are stepping into as you step out of something else. If the vision is not clear, it is far too easy to slip backward. Listing both the physical and psychological benefits of recovery made me realize just how much anorexia had stolen from my life. It gave me a daily focus of *all I could gain back* if I continued to pursue health and wholeness. Below is what I wrote on my recovery cards. Take note that not one of the benefits had anything to do with weight.

Physical Benefits: more color in my face, more energy, faster metabolism, more strength, defined muscles, better sleep, return of sex drive, ability to conceive and carry children, relief from constipation, looking less like a teenager and more like a woman, stronger bones, long life, better endurance, stronger nails, healthier hair and skin, return of typical blood pressure, happier disposition, improved concentration, regulated body temperature, ability to have a child biologically.

Psychological Benefits: happiness/excitement for life, ability to let loose and laugh, not so easily irritated, a better focus on God, stronger friendships, mentally able to parent children, not so tense, ability to eat out of the house with ease, much less preoccupation with food, realization that I am not required to be perfect, a better focus on others and their lives, healthier self-esteem, stronger bond with my husband, a return of my true self, positive attitude and emotions, appropriate expression of those emotions, a deep connectedness to others, spontaneity, better communication with my husband/parents/family, meaningful moments, respect for myself.

Did I cross over the TMI line mentioning constipation and sex? Maybe so. But here's what I know: anorexia's harm knows no borders, bodies and bedrooms included.

Act Your Way into Feeling

Otherwise known as "fake it till you make it," I realize this sounds a little cliché. Stick with me because there is so much truth here. I received this tip from Dr. J very early on in my therapy sessions. Remember, when I first started in recovery, I did not want to be there. I knew I needed to make serious changes, *but I did not want to make these changes.* My head and my heart were not in alignment. My head was pulling me forward, and my heart was pulling me backward, like a giant game of tug-of-war. This is common when you set out toward transformation.

If I had waited until I *felt* ready to act, ready to make a change, ready to gain weight, etc., it would have *never* happened. I had to bite the bullet, take that first baby step, and force myself to act. I had to push myself forward in stride, even when my heart was pushing me back into the life into which I had grown comfortable. But by taking each teeny-tiny step, eventually my actions were followed by genuine feelings. My feelings caught up to my actions.

After a few weeks of making whatever change I had incorporated, be it 2 percent milk or a cup of juice with breakfast, that change started to feel normal and part of my routine. Changes started to feel right, good, and *essential* for my improved well-being. And once one change became my new normal, it was that much easier to act, to take that next baby step toward another change that needed to happen. So continued a very healthy cycle.

Beautify Yourself

It might sound counterintuitive to include this tip to those trying to recover from a disease that focuses on outward appearance. But hear me out. When I started gaining my weight back, I had to do little non-weight-related things on a daily basis that made me feel beautiful. I got a fresh haircut, got a manicure or a pedicure on a (more) regular basis, bought a new great-smelling lotion, and spent time each day getting dressed, putting on makeup, and doing my hair. I realized there was a strong correlation between feeling put together and making actual progress on my goals. If I took the time each morning to invest in me, I was more likely to continue forward in my recovery. The days I allowed myself to sit around in my frumpy pajamas, sans makeup, with my hair in a messy bun? Those were the hardest days to follow my treatment plan and nutritional outline. I was much more likely to eat that scary high-calorie meal on the days I felt beautiful than on the days I did not. I am not suggesting this to an extreme, but take a few moments each day to invest in yourself.

Be Patient with Yourself As You Pursue God

During the darkest time of my eating disorder, I completely shut God out of my life. Sure, I still attended church and said casual prayers, but there was no intimate connection—no heart behind my action. I had closed the door on God and locked the deadbolt. So when it came time for recovery, naturally, I was mad at God. Mad that He allowed me to get so deep into the disease and mad that I now had to face my fears and take action. I silenced my voice and did not speak to Him about my recovery. I did not want to pray for guidance, read scripture for comfort, or carefully listen for any counsel He might provide. It saddens me to admit this, but this was the reality of my faith situation.

You know what? I think God understood, and still understands when we fall into these hard spaces. He knew I was not ready to embrace Him. He knew I was going to need some time. But all the while, He was right there waiting, just as He had been for the two years I chose anorexia over His loving freedom. And the more I acted my way into feeling and a new normal emerged, I found myself slowly longing to renew my relationship with the Lord.

Be patient with yourself. Be gentle. Telling God you aren't ready to talk to Him is still talking to Him. Warm and fuzzy spiritual feelings are not automatic when you sign the dotted line of recovery. If they are? Count yourself blessed. If not? Know you are absolutely normal, and in time your relationship with the Father will not only be found but will flourish.

Purge Your Closet

I know what you're thinking, and yes, this one is painful at first. But there is some deep psychological truth here. If we are going to take steps toward singing a new song, to fully embrace how God created us, it's time to purge the closet, friends. Today. Not next week or next month. Today. And by purge, I mean a relentless extermination of whichever clothes are holding you back from freedom.

When Dr. J suggested I do this, my immediate response was, "Well, I should probably keep them until they are snug, *and then* I will go shop for new clothes." Dr. J shot that idea down hardcore. So I went home and bagged up all the clothes that were already too small or should be too small and let them sit in the corner of my closet.

Baby steps, right? At least I was able to take my beloved 00s off hangers and put them out of immediate sight, or so I told myself. Yet, day after day, I would continue to reach for my favorite pair of jeans. Soon, as I continued to follow my meal plan and Dr. R's suggestions, these favorite jeans started getting tight, and I noticed a direct correlation in my mood. Trying to squeeze myself into jeans that cut off my circulation resulted in more crabbiness and irritation, if that was even possible. How Brandon put up with me, I will never know. He has indeed earned an extra special place in heaven. But it was then that I realized that my therapist was right. I had to get the clothes *out* of my closet once and for all.

On the day of my next therapy session, I bagged up all my unhealthy clothes, put them in the trunk of my car, and drove to my appointment. I admitted to Dr. J what I had done (not like she didn't know—therapists are so smart), and I promised that immediately after our appointment, I was taking the clothes to a donation center. That is exactly what I did.

So what is a girl to do who is in the midst of body changes with no clothes that fit? (My healthy clothes were still too big at that time.) Shop! Yep, my therapist gave me permission to shop it up until I had several items to wear that would fill the gap until my body returned to its healthy shape. This was one of the best decisions I made during early recovery. Wearing jeans with breathing room gave me the strength I needed to press on. And it eliminated the subtle taunting of those 00s.

I am not a math girl, but if I were, here is the formula I would use to break it all down:

Trying to gain weight + squeezing your body into clothes that do not fit = An intensified negative body image and a rotten attitude 24 hours a day.

Once I expanded my wardrobe, my pessimistic attitude began to lift. Out with the old and in with the new, if you will. I was able to live day-to-day, not focused on weight but focused on *life*. Focused on the good stuff!

Are there any clothes in your closet that you need to pass off? I'm giving you permission to unload the burden. Eliminate the source of unrest. The chances of this not working are less than 1 percent. I just made up that stat, but really, the risk of staying the same is so much greater here than the risk of change. Purge that closet. And know that I am right here, cheering you on.

Start Small

In the initial stages of recovery, securing professional help can feel more than overwhelming. Start small. You don't have to take on all the professionals at once, but start somewhere. This might mean that, like me, you hire a nutritionist first to set the pace and eventually work your way into therapy. Or vice versa. There is no right or wrong way to recover. Starting small is still starting, and that is a victory. Just as it takes time to warm back up to God, it takes time to grow comfortable working with a variety of professionals.

Create a Thankfulness Journal

It's been said that gratitude and anxiety cannot biologically occupy your thoughts at the same time. Tap into this blessing. Grab a journal, and at the end of every day, write down three things you are thankful for or three positive things that happened that day. They can be big or small. I found that after several weeks of starting my thankfulness journal, the momentum grew by leaps and bounds, and I was able to replace daily fear with daily points of joy-filled praise. When fear or anxiousness did creep in, I grabbed my journal and reviewed my blessings from days prior. I parked there for a while until all feelings of unrest left my mind and body.

You've got this, friends. It's a fight, but you aren't fighting alone. God leads the battle, and with Him there is always victory. You're walking the desert now, but beautiful manna and a grace-filled harvest await you on the other side. Dig deep. Press in. Triumph awaits.

In a thirteen-question body image survey to my blog readers, I asked the following question:

> *"If you could just give one tip to another woman for increasing her body-image confidence and embracing the true beauty in who God created her to be, what would it be?"* The answers I received were so rich with wisdom, I had to share some of them here.
>
> "Stay connected with people who have healthy walks with God! We were created to know Him and make Him known. It's no accident that isolation is used as a punishment in prisons. God desires for us to be in community, with Him and with each other."
>
> "Get the thoughts, whatever they are, out of your mind. Talking to yourself doesn't count. Write them out or verbalize them with someone you trust to not feed them back to you. If you hold onto them, alone in your mind, you will continue to believe you are not enough."
>
> "Remember that God didn't use a cookie cutter when He created us, and although there will be similarities, we aren't all supposed to look exactly alike. Just like we weren't all meant to be blonde, we weren't all meant to be a certain shape either. And also remember that a skinny body will do you no

good if it's not being fueled and used in a healthy manner."

"Be kind to yourself; don't tell yourself things that you wouldn't say to a friend or loved one."

"Throw out the scale and live a month without one single mirror in your house. Give it a try and see what happens. It's amazing!"

"Realize that we aren't here for ourselves; we are here to serve others and love others. I'd love for all women to just celebrate our beauty in *whatever* we are."

But the Cross

I wish I could say that since reaching my goal weight and ending therapy, I have never struggled with body image. But that would be a lie. I still get caught up in the rat race every now and then. While I no longer engage in unhealthy behaviors, there are still days I overanalyze how much I ate or why my pants are feeling a bit snug. I think that's okay. There is grace waiting for me, and for you, in those moments. We were never called to live perfectly, after all. So while there is not perfection, there is deep deliverance. I don't take that for granted.

Viewing ourselves and our bodies through the eyes of the cross is the only way we take the leap from dry desert to flourishing life. Jesus walked this earth to die a lowly death so that we could live perfectly imperfect lives with perfectly imperfect bodies. His blood on the cross seals an important promise; His blood signifies that He gave up His life for us, *just the way we are*. His death on that Friday allows us to embrace the freedom of that promise. He doesn't expect us to be anyone else or look like anyone else or have the body of anyone else. He urges us, in His Word, to lay these burdens down. Whatever these burdens might be, we are never expected to carry them on our own. We were never created to be that strong. "Praise be to the Lord, to God our Savior, who daily bears our burdens" (Psalm 68:19).

God desires deliverance for all His people today, just as He did for the Israelites in the Old Testament. And with that deliverance comes a new love song and our ability to sing. This is where it gets good because a new joy abounds. Our joy is renewed, and a new praise flows swiftly from our lips. We see this love song throughout chapter 15 of Exodus:

> Then Moses and the Israelites sang this song to the Lord: I will sing to the Lord, for he is highly exalted. The horse and its rider he has hurled into the sea. The Lord is my strength and my song; he has become my salvation. He is my God, and I will praise him, my father's God, and I will exalt him. (Exodus 15:1–2)

> Your right hand, O Lord, was majestic in power. Your right hand, O Lord, shattered the enemy. (Exodus 15:6)

> Who among the gods is like you, O Lord? Who is like you—majestic in holiness, awesome in glory, working wonders? (Exodus 15:11)

> In your unfailing love you will lead the people you have redeemed. In your strength you will guide them to your holy dwelling. (Exodus 15:13)

> Then Miriam the prophetess, Aaron's sister, took a tambourine in her hand, and all the women followed

her, with tambourines and dancing. Miriam sang to them: "Sing to the Lord, for he is highly exalted. The horse and its rider he has hurled into the sea." (Exodus 15:20–21)

Did you catch what happened in verses 20–21? I love this picture so much. Joy has returned. Beauty has filled the hearts of the people once again. And it's here we see Miriam and all the women with her give in to tambourine-playing and spirit-filled dancing.

Let us do the same, sweet sisters. Let's gently lay down whatever bodily expectations or frustrations hold us back from God's joyful song. You are worth so much more than a number. It's time to take up our tambourines once again. The world needs your voice. Today is the day. There is a beautiful song waiting to be sung. Yours just might be the most beautiful of all.

I can't help but wonder if the Israelites assumed that, since deliverance had occurred and God had freed them from bondage, the rest of life would be a walk in the park. That future struggles would not be a thing. That a testing of faith or a step on the battlefield wouldn't be required. I'm not sure. I do find it ironic that a mere two verses after the dancing has resumed and the tambourines are raised, we see the Israelites wandering the desert with nothing to quench their thirst.

> Then Moses led Israel from the Red Sea and they went into the Desert of Shur. For three days they traveled in the desert without finding water. When they came to Marah, they could not drink its water because it was bitter. (This is why the place is called Marah.) So the people grumbled against Moses, saying, "What are we to drink?" (Exodus 15:22–23)

Two verses later and praise is exchanged for grumbling. Did

they expect since life had been strenuous and rocky and twisted that life from here on out should always be easy? I am guilty of this assumption from time to time. But what the Lord is gently teaching me is this:

Sometimes life is just plain hard, and then, much to my surprise, it keeps getting harder.

What the Israelites didn't realize at the time is that, while God clearly parted the Red Sea to save their community, to bring the relief they so desperately needed, these same people would soon be required to wander the desert. Their faith journey had just begun.

I am not a clinical psychologist, registered dietitian, or in the medical field. I am just a woman who longs to share pieces of her story in hopes that they might, in some way, benefit others in need. If you are struggling with an eating disorder (or any other mental health concern), please seek the advice of licensed professionals.

Chapter 7

The Baby Itch

It was now May of 2010. I had nine months of recovery under my belt, and I was still making choices to heal my body physically, emotionally, and spiritually. I was on the rebound. I was starting to feel free—free from the heavy chains that had once confined me to the prison that is an eating disorder. I no longer met with my nutritionist but continued to meet with my therapist on a weekly basis.

By the grace of our powerful God, I was living and walking and breathing in the freedom God had always intended for me. Life was starting to feel a lot less complicated and a lot more joyful. It was around this time that Brandon and I started to discuss the idea of children. I was equally excited and nervous to embark on this next step of expanding our family. Excited because I had always dreamed of being a mother. Nervous because, even though I was in a much healthier spot physically, there was a high chance that the road to a baby would not be an easy one.

Anorexia Nervosa can inhibit a woman's fertility. When a woman's body weight becomes too low and goes into starvation mode, menstruation ceases because the body can no longer produce the hormones necessary to ovulate. Even when a woman has returned to a normal weight, the stress endured from the eating disorder can leave the body infertile. Doctors report that while some women's fertility is forever damaged, other women's bodies are able to push through and overcome, after initial medical intervention. Every woman, body, and bodily reaction is different.

Many choices that young women make related to their health and bodies can have tremendous consequences when it comes to fertility. It is well known that prior health and lifestyle choices can affect fertility. Women who are obese, smoke cigarettes or who have a history of STDs are more likely to suffer from infertility. But one issue that rarely gets attention when it comes to infertility yet can have lasting effects: eating disorders ... Women with eating disorders have abnormal eating patterns which affect their psychological and physical health. Some eat too much, some eat too little, and some go on a seemingly endless roller coaster of bingeing, purging, and starvation. While the incidence of EDs in the general population is 3–5%, a recent study found that at least 20% of women who sought treatment for infertility had a history of or current problem with EDs ... Ultimately, many women with EDs are likely to experience one or more of the following infertility issues: a loss of menstruation (permanent in 25% of women), uterine lining deficits, damaged oocytes (eggs) and diminished oocyte reserves. (Ivfconnections.com 2010)

Our eyes were fully open to the likelihood that our road to parenthood would not be a conventional one. I already knew this well before the baby itch set in. After the initial shock of seeing eighty-nine pounds on the scale the morning after Ike, these stats are what kept pushing me further and further into a healthier lifestyle. Hours upon hours had been spent researching the relationship between eating disorders and fertility/pregnancy, and that information kept me going on days I wanted to throw in the towel. Bottom line—I wanted to be a mom, and Brandon wanted to be a dad, and together we wanted to raise a family. And so, I would press on.

We decided not to actively try, but to no longer prevent pregnancy and just see what happened. What happened was four months passed and I had not one cycle. I previously mentioned that menstruation had ceased; this was actually me just guessing that menstruation had ceased. I had been on birth control the entire time, which of course we all know (except I didn't at the time because … clueless) produces a cycle in a woman regardless of her body's status of functionality. As my then gynecologist bluntly put it, "Brittnie, birth control would make my eighty-five-year-old grandma have a period." *Well, okay then. Thanks for the visual.* Her point was that for the past several years, while I was technically having a monthly cycle, I was only having one because fake hormones were forcing my body to work. Not because my body was in working order. So take away the hormones, and you take away your cycle. You're welcome for that short, eye-opening biology lesson.

As much as I knew that medical intervention was a possibility, deep down I expected that everything would be okay. That maybe by praying boldly enough and hard enough, God would just flip my body into gear. That God would just shower the grace and let us scamper over this consequence of my sin. I came to the table expecting that my genuine remorse and heart change would be enough to let us skip the label of "infertile." That expectation was not my reality.

Labs were ordered and blood work drawn, and the news was not at all what I wanted to hear. The doctor shared that there was nothing she could do to help. *What? Isn't that, like, what you do? I have known several people who turned to their gynecologist for pills and patches to help boost fertility! There must be a way.*

She tenderly told me that, unfortunately, my body was past the point of responding to the type of treatments she administered. There was proof in the numbers. My hormones were too low, some nonexistent, and thus my body would not respond to the medicine she could prescribe.

I was given a diagnosis of hypothalamic amenorrhea. (The hypothalamus in the center of the brain, which signals the release of specific hormones needed for reproduction, was basically dormant.) And I was told that if we were ready to have a baby, I would need to seek the counsel of a fertility specialist. She suggested we begin immediately. I left that appointment with an unsettling diagnosis and an extra heavy heart.

Real Talk: Has there ever been a time when, despite what you knew to be reality, you expected God to pull through for you anyway? A time when you expected Him to overcome the odds, but He decided it better to be still? Think back on this situation and the emotions you experienced.

Action Steps: Thinking on this same scenario, journal your thoughts and include any unexpected blessings that might have come from God's decision to sit and be still instead of act. Dig deep. There is always a blessing to be found, even if walking the desert.

A Journey Down the Off-Beaten Path

I left that appointment with my head hung low and a shiny purple folder of infertility material I didn't want to read through. That night, as Brandon and I discussed the information and our options, we decided it would be best to start the process. After all, there was no guarantee of the process going smoothly or swiftly. We prayed. We cried. And I apologized, over and over again. Because it seemed clear that it was my selfish choices, my worship of self, that was taking us down this off-beaten path.

I will never forget what he said to me in that moment. "Britt, you are going to have to let it go. It is what it is, but I don't blame you, and I'm not upset with you. Neither is God. This might be a consequence of past choices, but God isn't dwelling on what was, and neither should we. Your past is in the past, and it is time to move forward in confidence." He was so right. Satan had the opportunity to plant guilt in my heart. Satan's hope was that if I took back the guilt and watered it diligently, it would fester and grow and bloom into a different type of destruction. I couldn't let him win again. I had to let it go and move forward in faith.

Our appointment with the fertility specialist, Dr. G, went as expected. The doctor confirmed my gynecologist's suspicion that typical fertility drugs would not work in my situation. Dr. G laid out our options and gave his suggestions. Sitting in the office that day, I received more information about reproduction than one would ever care to know. Except I did care because the goal was pregnancy.

But between the diagrams and words like *hysteroscopy, injections, follicles, cysts,* and a breakdown of the mile-long list of medications I would need to order, my head was spinning. Oh, and once I started on the medications, I would need to come back every two to three days for a blood draw and follicle scan. I was initiated into this world of infertility, and it was all I could do to keep a smile on my face and a "thank you" on my lips.

The next year was filled with lots of injectable medicine and needles and blood work and follicle scans and canceled cycles and consultations and updated treatment plans and disappointments.

After what felt like eleven months of constant roadblocks, I couldn't believe the day had finally arrived: the day of our IVF embryo transfer. Today was the day I could possibly become pregnant. I could hardly think straight, and it was all I could do to keep myself busy and distracted before the scheduled procedure. I drank my two liters of water, popped my Valium as instructed, and waited to be called back. I changed into my gown, and Brandon into his marshmallow jumpsuit, and the nurses lead us back to the operating room. We were seconds away from the desire of our hearts. The nurses, laughing jovially, explained that in a few seconds, I would be considered PUPO (pregnant until proven otherwise). I lay there waiting with expectancy.

The doctor entered the room, and by his demeanor, I could tell something was not right. In a matter of minutes, the conversation turned serious. Dr. G. explained all the possible and highly likely risks to my body if we were to transfer even a single embryo. *Excuse me, what? Are you serious? Are we really having this conversation as I am lying here seconds away from seeing my little embryos planted into my uterus?* I lay there thinking I was on the craziest episode ever in the history of *Punk'd,* and Ashton Kutcher was going to jump out from around the corner (also in his white marshmallow jumpsuit), and then we would all laugh and get on with business. But this wasn't a cruel episode of *Punk'd,* and Ashton never made an appearance.

Dr. G explained that my ovaries were severely inflamed and the follicles that were not retrieved during the egg retrieval procedure several days earlier were still growing with a vengeance. Proceeding with even a single embryo transfer could put me at risk, again, for ovarian hyper-stimulation syndrome (in the most severe of cases, OHSS can be life-threatening).

The choice was ours. Emotions high, we had to decide to either take that risk or do nothing. And doing nothing that day meant another two-month process to prepare my body for a frozen embryo transfer cycle. Two months, when you have already waited eleven months, feels like an eternity. I looked at Brandon and, sobbing through my tears, said, "Please make the call. I trust you. I am too emotional to make a good decision."

That is when the Dr. G looked deep into Brandon's eyes and disclosed, "If this was my wife, I wouldn't let her do it." And with that, the decision was made. Ten minutes later, I changed into my regular clothes and was wheeled to the car in a wheelchair from a procedure that hadn't happened.

I sat in church the following Sunday and tried to push feelings of bitterness aside. I was supposed to be on bedrest, after all—not in church. But there I sat after one more disappointment on what felt like an endless journey of heartbreak. God had parted my Red Sea and set me free from the slavery of anorexia, but my time in the desert was far from over. It was like manna from heaven was there taunting me and then forcefully ripped away. Like how the Israelites finally landed on water, but soon realized they couldn't reap its benefits as the water was too bitter. What a tease!

"When they came to Marah, they could not drink its water because it was bitter. (This is why the place is called Marah.) So the people grumbled against Moses, saying, 'What are we to drink?'" (Exodus 15:22–23).

How much longer would I wander this dry land? How much longer would the water be undrinkable? When would I get my tambourine dance?

As our preacher began his sermon, I couldn't help but assume it was written specifically for me. This is what I heard that day ... "God does not put us through trials to oppress us but to stretch us." He was stretching me, all right. He was stretching me to handle more than I ever thought possible. He was stretching me to love deeper and give bigger and practice more patience and empathy with others. He was stretching my marriage (for the better). He was stretching me to know that regardless of my plans and dreams and expectations, He was the only constant. He was the only master planner. His stretching allowed more of me to cling to Him.

And that is what life is all about really, isn't it? Clinging to God in each and every happy, sad, joyful, unexpected, and tearful moment? So while I was still heartsick from the letdown of a failed procedure, I could rejoice in knowing that God was not my oppressor—He was my stretcher. That, my friends, is a song always worth singing.

When a woman is in the process of IVF, and specifically a frozen embryo transfer (likely due to the risk of OHSS), she is introduced to a new medicine—progesterone in oil (PIO). If I had to rate PIO on a scale of 1 being "doesn't hurt at all" and 10 being "the worst pain of my life," PIO would easily be a 20. I still don't think my backside has forgiven me. I wrote the following on my blog on August 29, 2011. I was in dire need of some comic relief.

Dear Progesterone in Oil,

Oh how I loathe you. From day one, you have not been nice to me. Here I am, asking for your help, and you just laugh in my face. The nurses warned me about you. Oh yes, they told me you would be painful, cause my backside to swell, turn a devil red, and form welts the size of large strawberries. You might think it is funny that you cause me to walk like an eighty-year-old woman, but really it's not. I hate to sit down because your after-effects Never. Ever. Go. Away. You are like the mean girls I avoided in middle school. I bet you are secretly talking to them (you know who they are!) and informing them of your tortuous ways. Follistim was a lot cooler than you, and I mean this literally. You make me sweat, especially at night, as I lie wide-awake from your insomnia-inducing ways. Why do you have to be so thick, and why is your needle (seriously) two inches long? That is totally unnecessary. I say this with the love of Jesus, but you totally suck. Why can't I inject you in my thigh or an area of my backside that has some extra skin? Seriously, the intramuscular portion of my bottom was a bad call on your part. Who wants to shoot themselves in their booty muscle? Enough said.

Regardless of our relationship the past eleven days, I will not give up on you. Deep down I know your heart is good and you are just trying to support me and my goals of motherhood. So because of this, I will not post crazy YouTube videos of myself injecting you. Yes, you should take a look online because there are some crazies out there who actually video themselves shooting their booty up for the world to see. Who does that? Instead, I will continue to stick out our friendship day after day. I won't ever leave you waiting so you don't have to worry about me standing you up. I will be there at nine o'clock every single night or until Dr. G tells me otherwise. See you in T-minus five minutes.

Love,
Brittnie

Through all the blood (literally), sweat (literally), and tears (literally), our infertility journey came to an end on September 8, 2011. After what felt like my five hundredth blood draw and a five-hour wait, the nurses called me at work, and I then called Brandon at work (such a glamorous way to get the news, no?) to confirm that yes, a baby was on the way. Or possibly two babies. My HCG BETA count was over three thousand, and three days later, it was over five thousand, too high to record. And a few days after that? I cried messy tears of joy and Brandon cried messy tears of panic as we stared at two beautiful babies on that blessed ultrasound machine. A few days after that? The most breathtaking sound ... two beating hearts.

At eight weeks of pregnancy, two beating hearts turned into one beating heart. Baby A didn't have the stamina to thrive or survive. Baby A's heart was averaging only 85 bpm, much too slow. And eventually, it just stopped. I was by myself that day, the day when we learned Baby A was no longer with us. I drove myself to work, crying tears of sadness and thanksgiving, pain and peace, bitterness and delight.

I've learned you can be in that place of dual emotions, holding two opposites in your heart at the exact same time. So much sadness surrounding the baby who had left us, yet so much elation surrounding the baby who still lived in my womb.

Baby B, Clara Anne Blackburn, was born healthy in May of the following year. She was tiny and beautiful and perfect, and I was quickly initiated into the group of newbie mothers who are on cloud nine but have *absolutely no clue* on God's good earth what they are doing. Can I get an amen?

Thinking back over our infertility journey, I am reminded of so many other women, maybe even you, who are balancing the dance of eager expectation and disheartening disappointment, month after month after month. Negative test after negative test. Failed procedure after failed procedure. Trying to believe the promise that with God, all things are possible (Matthew 19:26), yet feeling like maybe that promise was for everyone else. Like He has thrown us in this desert land and then left us to fend for ourselves.

Come really close for a second, will you? While I know you're at the end of your rope and feel you have nothing left to give, please don't give up on Him. It might feel like He no longer cares about you and the desires of your heart. I've been there. But His promises are for each and every one of us, not just some of us, and they are ours for the claiming! He does care about your desires, so very much. Lay it all out, talk to Him, and trust Him through the stretching.

Remember that He is not in the business of oppression. God does not ask us to walk anywhere He hasn't already walked himself. God himself spent time in the desert. He experienced deep thirst and cried out for a drink. Every situation or sadness or setback? He has been there. He knows the pain. He's walked that walk. And He knows the joy and beauty that lie on the other side.

Let's claim that joy, friends. Let's learn from the Israelites and choose praise over grumbling, regardless of how long our desert walk might be. He's reserved a tambourine for each of us.

Real Talk: Do you feel like God is oppressing you or holding out on you in any way? How is God stretching you in this season?

Action Step: Pray. Pray for whatever expectation you currently hold in your heart. Pray that God will open your eyes to see the beauty in the stretching. Pray that He will fill your heart with abundant joy, despite what feels like a never-ending desert walk.

"For the eyes of the Lord are on the righteous, and his ears are attentive to their prayer." (1 Peter 3:12)

"Surely the arm of the Lord is not too short to save, nor his ear to dull to hear." (Isaiah 59:1)

To read the detailed account of our infertility journey, visit http://ajoyrenewed.blogspot.com/p/fertility-journey.html.

Chapter 8

A Different Kind of Beautiful

D espite the sleeplessness that comes with having a newborn, I enjoyed my transition to working full-time in the home. It was a shock to the system at first, as is any big life change, and there were many days I questioned if I was cut out for this gig. But over time, the dust settled and our new normal arrived.

Clara's newborn days were lovely ... well, besides the colic that lasted from week six to week twelve, and the sleep that did not exist until month six. But we played and explored the world together and took lots of daytime naps to offset the exhaustion. I felt like the luckiest woman in the world; it was pure bliss.

It was around Clara's four-month birthday that we realized she was different. E-mails would arrive in my inbox from Baby Center or TheBump.com. titled, "Your four-month-old's development," and it was clear our girl was lagging behind. Having a social work background, I was also tuned in to these delays.

At Clara's four-month well check with the pediatrician, Dr. O lovingly commented on her own observations, confirming my suspicion that something was a little off. Yet Dr. O told us not to worry too much right now, as it was still too early to make assumptions. We would wait until Clara's six-month well check and reevaluate.

Six months rolled around, and nothing had changed. My girl was not making eye contact, not smiling socially, not babbling, not imitating gestures or facial expressions, and not engaging in infant games such as peek-a-boo. When I would try to get her attention, it was as if she was looking past me, as if no one was home. Clara's fine and gross motor skills were delayed. She was not using her hands functionally (such as banging or reaching for objects during play) or sitting up unassisted. Walking into her six-month well check, I was mentally prepping for what I knew was to come. My mom came with me (my parents had also been concerned for several months), and we sat in on a well check exam that I will never forget, an exam that every parent prays against.

What I loved about Dr. O was she began every exam with, "What's on your mind?" This gave me the opportunity to restate any worries instead of being immediately bombarded with her concerns. Dr. O tenderly agreed that Clara was delayed in all areas and a plan of action was needed. If we waited much longer to "see if things resolve," we would be missing a prime window of brain development. I agreed that a liberal plan was the best plan in this situation. I walked away with a referral to a neurologist, Early Childhood Intervention, and options for physical therapy, occupational therapy, and eventual speech therapy.

Something deep down in my soul told me we were in this for the long haul. In that moment, I knew this would be a lifelong desert journey, not a three-day stay or a forty-year visit (Exodus 16:34).

By the time Clara turned nine months, we were knee-deep in appointments, consultations, blood draws, therapy sessions, and a wide variety of hypotheses to answer the central question: what is the underlying cause of Clara's global developmental delays? As a way to process all that we were going through, and as a way to remember the fine details, I wrote a letter to my baby girl.

Dear sweet Clara,

I can hardly put into words how much joy you bring to our lives. You light up the world around you, and each day is such a blessing. Your smile is contagious and completely melts our hearts. You are developing your own little personality, which is so fun to watch.

You just turned nine months old. I cannot believe it! Where does the time go? As you know, about three months ago, at your six-month well check, Dr. O let us know that she had some concerns with your delayed development, both physically and socially. At that time, you were not really making much eye contact, smiling, babbling, laughing, or tracking things with your eyes. You did not seem too interested in engaging with me or Daddy or the world around you. You liked to hang your head down instead of looking up. At that time, you were also not sitting up on your own.

Dr. O talked with us about some steps we could take to check things out, just to be proactive in helping you meet your milestones and to see if there was any reason why you might be lagging a bit behind your baby friends. Dr. O suggested we get you in occupational therapy and that we meet with a baby brain doctor, called a neurologist, Dr. R.

We met with Dr. R for the first time in December 2012. He confirmed that you were showing signs of developmental delays, and he also said that your head is a lot smaller than babies your age. He said you have Microcephaly. Because of these two things, he wanted to run lots of tests and also get some of your blood.

Mommy and Daddy were a little overwhelmed leaving that appointment. We had so many questions and shed some tears, but we knew that God was holding our little family in His hands. We were not fearful, just overwhelmed and a little nervous with all this new information.

You had a hearing test done not too long after that appointment, and you did not pass in either ear. This was a repeat of the same test they did in the hospital when you were a few days old. Because of this, you had a more extensive test done, called an ABR (Auditory Brainstem Response), where you had to be put to sleep so the ear doctor could monitor your brain activity. She put little stickers on your head (called electrodes) that measured your brain's response to a little clicking sound. Clara, you passed with flying colors! You showed no signs of hearing loss at all! Mommy and Daddy joked that you were just trying to keep us on our toes. Silly girl.

You had your eyes checked, and other than already being nearsighted, the doctor saw no concerns with your vision. We were so thankful!

The neurologist did a little test on you called the Batelle Developmental Inventory, when you were about eight months, and the test confirmed his suspicions that your development was lagging several months behind. Based on your results, Dr. R guessed that you would probably start to walk around age two. This made mommy cry, but then I realized, who cares when you start to walk? You have your whole life to walk, so it's really no big deal.

71

You had to get lots of blood drawn just so we could investigate a little further. These were not fun days for any of us, but overall you were so strong! Two different times you hardly even cried! Your regular lab work came back fine.

Dr. R also ran some genetic tests (they are big words—a Chromosomal Microarray Analysis, Rett Syndrome, and Fragile X Syndrome) to see if these might be the reasons you were a little behind and your head a little small. A nurse took your blood and then it was sent to a lab where it was watched carefully and put under a microscope. They found that you are missing a portion of your fourth chromosome (the part you are missing is 4p15.32). This is called a chromosome abnormality, or some people call it a genetic deletion since you are missing some genetic material. Dr. R is not quite sure what this means yet, or if it even matters! Genetic testing is so new that the research base is still somewhat limited. Last week the Fragile X test came back negative! We were so thankful! We are still waiting on the results of the Retts test and one additional test (that has to do with metabolic function since Dr. R said 4p15.32 is involved with how your little body metabolizes different things). We are praying that you do not have Retts, but if you do, you better believe this will not change one thing about our love for you. You are perfect, no matter what the results show.

A few weeks ago, you had an MRI done on your brain. You had to be put to sleep for this too, just like the ABR test, except this time they had to give you an IV in your foot. It took a while to get the needle in your foot, but once they got it in and gave you the sleep medicine, you did great. The results show that all the major parts of your brain are just as they should be! Dr. R did mention that certain areas of your brain are not as myelinated as most babies your age, but it is still within a normal range of abnormal so he is not too concerned right now. He would like to have another MRI done in a few years to make sure it has resolved. Praise God that all the parts of your brain are there! Dr. R mentioned that while your brain is small compared to other babies, it is filling up your headspace appropriately so that is a huge blessing!

You started seeing an occupational therapist (who works in Dr. R's office) once a week (December 2012), and you are making great progress. Clara, after just one week of OT, you started sitting up on your own. The OT, Ms. Brittany, is working on getting your back and neck muscles super strong. She says this will help you meet your milestones. She is also helping you become more aware of your hands. She gives us lots and lots of homework exercises to do each day, and you seem to really enjoy our little playtime. Ms. Brittany is blown away by your progress week after week. You bring her so much joy, and she loves playing with you. The OT session is one of our favorite times of the week. It is so fun to watch you blossom. You amaze us. Oh, and last week, you went from lying on your back/ tummy to sitting up on your own in your bed! You have only done it once, but we are sure you will do it again soon.

You have another friend who works for ECI (Early Childhood Intervention), Ms. Misty, who comes once a week to play with you at our house. She started coming in January 2013 and is called a Specialized Skills Trainer. The three of us sit on the floor and play together. She also gives us exercises to work on between visits. She is so happy with your progress so far and thinks you are beyond cute! ECI will work with us until we are ready to stop services, or until you hit three years old. Once you are one year, they will send a physical therapist and speech therapist to our house to work with you.

At this point, we have pretty much finished most of the major testing. Mommy and Daddy are going to talk with a team of people at Texas Children's Hospital, called geneticists, who will give us more information about the part of chromosome that you are missing. They might want to take some of Mommy and Daddy's blood to see if we are also missing 4p15.32. We go in May, just after you turn one year old!

Clara, we want you to know that our love for you is unconditional. It doesn't matter what any of these tests show or what the doctors say might happen in the future. You were created perfectly, in God's image, and no diagnosis will change that.

You are a joy to us. Every day I hold you and ask myself, "How did I get this lucky?" Yes, we have a lot going on, and our days can sometimes be really busy and stressful, but I would not change a thing about our time together. I am so thankful I am able to be at home with you right now. I love watching you grow and blossom, and I am eager to see how God uses you (though small) to do big things. We love you so much. I can't say that enough.

Yesterday at your nine-month well check, Dr. O. stated, "It is obvious that Clara has been blessed with the perfect mom and dad to meet all her needs."

I replied, "No. Actually, this mom and dad have been blessed with the perfect Clara."

Love,
Mommy (and Daddy)

Special Girl, Special Calling

It turned out that the geneticists were not at all concerned with Clara's chromosome deletion, as the portion she was missing was very small and likely not linked to any specific disorder or cause of concern. Like water to a parched soul, we clung to this news and savored it for what it was: good news. But while they were not concerned by the chromosome abnormality, the team of geneticists were concerned with the following: Clara's head size (microcephaly), delays in both motor and language skills, dysmorphic facial features—specifically her unibrow, sunken eyes, and ear shape. They were also concerned by her small, repetitive behaviors, such as shaking of the head or flapping of the hands, and her sensory sensitivities to light and noise.

The geneticists agreed that these concerns were symptoms of something. They just didn't know what that something was yet. To further investigate, more blood was needed. Holding my baby down and enduring her screams as vial after vial was filled was not my idea of a good time. I don't think I made it through a blood draw without crying some tears myself. But this test, the Whole Genome Sequencing, was our best shot at a firm diagnosis, a reason behind all of our concerns. The geneticists kept repeating, "I really think we will find something."

Since this test required blood from all three of us, the doctors would also be able to tell us what percentage of a chance there was that any future children would also carry the same struggles. Once blood was drawn, it would take at minimum five months to obtain results. *Five. Months.* Five months felt like an eternity to this first-time mama who faced daily the reality that her child was different. Five months of wondering and stressing and questioning all the what-ifs: *What if it's really bad? What if they don't find anything? What if all children are guaranteed the same diagnosis?*

During this five-month wait, Clara, at thirteen months, started displaying an odd twitch-like behavior, usually while eating, but sometimes even when sitting in our laps or playing on the floor. When eating, the twitch was followed by intense coughing and gagging. This was not only unusual but also scary to watch. Our neurologist ordered an EEG to rule out the possibility of seizures and referred us to a pulmonary doctor to make sure she wasn't aspirating (common in kids who had reflux as an infant). One EEG and swallow study later (insurance was loving us by this time!), and we were given no new news. Which was a blessing. And also quite frustrating.

When you're in the thick of symptoms and struggles and blood draws and testing, you hit this point of just wanting an answer, regardless of what that answer is. You hit this point where you just want to know what you're dealing with so you can address it and move on. I am sure so many of you can relate. There comes a point when you are no longer scared of a diagnosis because a diagnosis could pave the way for the most appropriate treatment plan. It was in this five-month wait that my heart shifted toward this new way of thinking. I was no longer scared of the answer. I craved the answer. But that craving did not negate intense moments of emotional breakdown.

At fifteen months, we saw an Autism specialist, and Clara was given a diagnosis of Autism. The doctor was frank in admitting that yes, she was a bit young to diagnose, but she presented with all of the symptoms. Could there be more to the story? Yes. But did she fit all diagnostic criteria for Autism? Yes. It was there I was thankful for the mental shift that had occurred in my brain because if not, I probably would have packed us up and slammed the door.

Clara's fifteen-month well check rolled around, so off we went to the pediatrician. And by *we*, I mean me, Clara, and the surprise baby in my womb. I was four months along at the time, but the news was still fresh. I didn't find out I was pregnant until ten weeks' gestation. Yes, ten weeks. I know. When you spend month after month shooting yourself up with medicine to conceive the first time around, you don't give much thought to the extra fatigue or extra hunger because how in the world would conceiving a child be so easy as just being intimate with your spouse? Such a crazy concept. Anyway, that day I remember feeling particularly strong, a sense of deep contentment running through my bones. I walked into that appointment, head held high, holding my baby who, regardless of struggles, I was so very proud to call mine.

Every well check begins with the nurse asking a series of questions to the parent, an easy way to screen for any concerns. This day was no different. I was prepared for this interaction, but I was not prepared for my reaction.

Nurse: *Does your child say three to five words?*

Me: *No.*

Nurse: *Does your child follow simple instructions, such as, "Bring me the ball?"*

Me: *No.*

Nurse: *Does your child drink from a sippy cup?*

Me: *No.*

> *Nurse: Can your child feed, or attempt to feed, herself with a spoon?*

> *Me: No.*

> *Nurse: Does your child point to objects in a book with one finger?*

> *Me: No.*

> *Nurse: Does your child understand how items are used, such as using, or attempting to use, a brush to brush her hair?*

> *Me: No.*

> *Nurse: Can your child scribble with a crayon?*

> *Me: No.*

> *Nurse: Is your child walking?*

> *Me: No.*

And in that moment, all the guardedness washed away, and I flooded the floor with my tears. Imagine the emotional meltdown of all meltdowns, and you have a fairly accurate picture. That poor nurse. She didn't even know what hit her.

> *Nurse: I'm sorry, these are just all questions I have to ask.*

> *Me: I know and I understand. She's just really delayed, so most all of these questions will probably not apply to us. Can we just skip the rest?*

On most days, I feel strong and confident and not weighed down by the delays my sweet girl is experiencing. I get used to what our normal is, and just roll with it. But not that day. That day, as the nurse ran through the questions, Clara sat on the examination table, struggling to play with a wooden puzzle. All the senses combined (visually watching her struggle, audibly hearing the questions, and verbally speaking her delays) were too much. I still have moments like this, moments when I so deeply want to answer, "Yes!" but the truth is revealed in too many nos. There are bound to be many more days like these in my future of parenting Clara, and my future in general.

Emotions don't make us weak; they just make us human.

Wherever you are in your journey, be it developmental delays or job loss or mental illness or marriage struggles or financial burdens or infertility or a wide-open life resume that you just don't know how God will fill, let yourself feel it. Let the tears flow when they need to flow and trust that God will work in the midst of your mess. Trust that even when every answer is a no, the Lord himself will use it for a greater good.

> *Our nos turn into His yesses, and His yesses turn into kingdom work.*

And kingdom work as a result from my wilderness wandering? I can't think of a better gift.

Because of the extravagance of those revelations, and so I wouldn't get a big head, I was given the gift of a handicap to keep me in constant touch with my limitations. Satan's angel did his best to get me down; what he in fact did was push me to my knees. No danger then of walking around high and mighty! At first I didn't think of it as a gift, and begged God to remove it. Three times I did that, and then he told me, My grace is enough; it's all you need. My strength comes into its own in your weakness. Once I heard that, I was glad to let it happen. I quit focusing on the handicap and began appreciating the gift. It was a case of Christ's strength moving in on my weakness. Now I take limitations in stride, and with good cheer, these limitations that cut me down to size—abuse, accidents, opposition, bad breaks. I just let Christ take over! And so the weaker I get, the stronger I become. 2 Corinthians 12:7-10 (The Message 2002)

The phone rang about 9:00 a.m. that day ...

"Mrs. Blackburn, this is Texas Children's Genetics. Dr. L would like you and your husband to come in as soon as possible. Can you be here this Thursday at 10:00 a.m.?"

"Yes, of course. But we had an appointment for early January to discuss the test results, and it's only November. Does this mean they found something?"

"I cannot confirm or deny, but Dr. L specifically asked that I call to bring you in this week."

I slowly put down the phone and sat my body on the cold, kitchen tile. Deep down, I knew. They had found something. They had found a reason for my daughter's delays, and I was just not sure what to do in that moment. *It takes months upon months to get an appointment with this team of doctors, and they* are *bringing us in this week? How bad is it?* I wondered. *What are they going to tell us? What does this mean for the baby girl in my womb? Will she be affected too?* I rubbed my seven-month-pregnant belly, but my hands were the only part of my body I could physically put into motion. Just seconds before, my spirit was light and free, and with one short phone call, my spirit felt heavy and burdensome. One phone call can change everything.

We knew going in that if there was a firm reason behind Clara's struggles, this test would find it. The Whole Genome Sequencing is the best of the best. The head honcho of head honchos. The Big Kahuna. When both our pediatrician and neurologist looked at us and said, "If the geneticists are recommending this test, and your insurance will pay for it, you don't question. You do the test," we knew it was our best shot at an accurate diagnosis.

(United Health Care, I am forever grateful. It is obvious we were not your favorite customers that year, or ever, but spending 10K on our girl was worth it. It was worth every phone delay and messed-up claim and every time we heard, "We apologize for the delay. A representative will be with you shortly.")

On November 21, 2013, we received Clara's diagnosis of Cohen Syndrome. The results were black and white. She had a mutation in both copies of the VPS13B gene, located on chromosome eight. Cohen Syndrome is a *very rare* autosomal recessive genetic disease (fewer than one thousand cases worldwide, although this number is growing as newer technology allows children to be accurately diagnosed at an earlier age) that affects motor skills and intellectual development.

Individuals who have a faulty gene copy on one chromosome and a working copy of that gene on the other chromosome are carriers. Carriers for the great majority of conditions due to autosomal recessive changes are usually not affected by the genetic condition. Although only one of the gene copies is working, the cell can usually still work at this reduced amount. Yet when two carriers of the same faulty gene have a child (Brandon and me), each parent has a chance of passing on either the faulty gene or the working copy of the gene to that child. There is a one in four chance (25 percent) that they will have a child who inherits both copies of the faulty gene from his or her parents. In this case, no working gene product will be produced, and the child will be affected by the condition. This is the case in Clara, who inherited both copies of the faulty gene from Brandon and me, responsible for her Cohen Syndrome. Any future child born to us has a 25 percent chance of being affected by the disorder.

As Dr. L began to explain the symptoms of Cohen Syndrome, it all started to make sense: global developmental delays, Microcephaly, large range of joint movement, extreme nearsightedness, increased susceptibility to illness, sensory issues (coupled with Autistic-like behaviors), and other identifying features, such as her thick hair and unibrow. Everything fit. All children with Cohen Syndrome fall on a spectrum (much like Autistic children). Some develop fairly well and can function more independently, while others do not. Some walk and talk, and some never take a first step or utter a word. Some have perfect vision, and some experience intense degeneration of the retina (eventually leading to night blindness). Some are severely affected by neutropenia (a lower-than-average number of white blood cells), which makes them more prone to infection and sickness, while others seem to have a higher tolerance for illness. Most all children with Cohen Syndrome, though, take *a very long time* to meet any and every developmental milestone; however, once a milestone is achieved, there is no regression. We are so thankful for this piece of an extremely complex puzzle. I hold onto this piece of hope on days when hope feels out of reach.

We walked out of Dr. L's office with a new diagnosis, but with the same baby girl. She had an unfamiliar label, but she was no different.

If you are that mama, the mama with the child who lags behind or with a fresh diagnosis, I want to share a little secret that saved me and continues to save me time and time again: A diagnosis is not a prognosis. I will say it again.

A diagnosis is not a prognosis.

A diagnosis is an analysis, a conclusion based on facts and findings, but it is not a prophecy. A diagnosis will point you in the right direction and give clues about the future, but it does not encompass your child's future.

That day in Dr. L's office, we learned that children with Cohen's typically walk between age two and five, speak first words between age one and five, and speak in sentences between age five and six.

About 20 percent of children fail to develop verbal language. That was, and is, Clara's diagnosis, but these trends are not stamped in stone. Don't succumb to the stamping. Through endless amounts of therapeutic intervention (up to three therapy sessions a day), Clara began crawling at age fourteen months and walking at twenty-three months, exactly two weeks before she turned two years old.

So keep fighting, mama of the newly diagnosed child. Keep pushing the limits. Resist the urge to let the locusts in to roam free and eat away whatever green remains in you, your child, and your family (Exodus 10:15). Because your child needs you. Your family needs you. They need your hope and your joy to fight the wilderness. They feed off your perspective. And with hope and joy securely intact, any diagnosis is bound to be a perfect one.

Fixed Eyes

It is so easy to get stuck in all the "what ifs" and "she cant's" and "may not evers" of Clara's development. I am faced daily with the reality of our situation and see with my eyes, on repeat, all the ways Clara lags behind her peers.

At nearly five years old, she has never uttered a word. She doesn't babble like a young infant. If I'm comparing her language on a developmental scale, she might equal a six-month-old, maybe. When I find her crying, she has no way of telling me what is wrong. When sick, she can't tell me what hurts. She doesn't play with toys functionally or interact with her peers when in a social setting. She is slowly learning how to use the toilet. She can't feed herself with utensils and doesn't typically respond to her name. When transitioning from room to room or outdoors to indoors, she requires physical guidance, as she doesn't understand or follow basic directives. The intensity of her sensory issues wax and wane; thus, events deemed fun by a typical child have the potential to exponentially heighten Clara's stress level (think birthday parties, the zoo, restaurants, a children's museum).

She most likely won't be able to live independently. She will need assistance, forever, with daily tasks, such as bathing and grooming and dressing. Dreams such as walking across a graduation stage or across the altar to meet her groom might never come to fruition.

But that is just the thing—these are my dreams, not hers. All she knows is what she knows. And while we will always push her to reach her full potential and skill set, she is perfectly content to be just as God created her. Anyone who spends two seconds around Clara immediately sees peace and joy and love and beauty, not the disappointment of not living the life she could be living. It is when I get cemented in all the negatives, all the disappointments, that my hope starts to hide and my joy starts to fade. A new way of thinking, which is only fair to my girl, is to zone in on all the "she cans." It's the simple (but very hard) switch from negative to positive language. Replacing the weak with the strong. Not denying the struggles, but dwelling on the victories.

So how do we do this? How do we shift our thinking and the focus of our eyes?

First, we let ourselves grieve the loss. A special needs child is not the type of child I envisioned when dreaming of a family. A rare genetic syndrome was not part of my family plan. Some of you are probably nodding your heads in agreement.

Coming to terms and accepting our children's lives for what they are starts by letting ourselves feel the pain of disappointment. We must allow ourselves into this dark space to make room for the light on the other side. It is easy to push aside feelings of grief in the name of "moving forward," or "getting our children the best care possible," or "not wasting any time for the sake of our children's development." Oh goodness, how I did this very thing. We can only move forward for so long, but then the loss must be dealt with. We grieve so we can press on in hope. We grieve so we can sing a new song when singing doesn't seem logical. We face the reality of our situation, that our desert stay will indeed last a lifetime, by sitting in our sadness.

But we continue, head held high, because *grief is vital but not a place to call our forever home.* We can choose to dwell on what could have been or move forward in trust and embrace what is—and what is, is an amazingly beautiful, spirited, loving, joy-filled daughter I get to call mine.

Parenthood is about raising and celebrating the child you have, not the child you thought you'd have. It's about understanding your child is exactly the person they are supposed to be. And, if you're lucky, they might be the teacher who turns you into the person you're supposed to be. (Ryan 2010)

Clara's life, my parenting of her, is so much different than I ever expected. But living in the world of my expectations equals living in a world of constant frustration and disappointment. I must fix my eyes on Jesus, not on the can'ts or probably won'ts. It is when the Israelites focused on the water they didn't have, the food they couldn't taste, that their joy escaped and their attitude turned sour. The same is true for me. Clara's life still holds an endless amount of beauty, even in the midst of her differences.

By embracing her life for what it is, not what it could have been, I experience a deep joy that most parents never have the opportunity to experience. What a blessing! My bitter water has turned sweet! (Exodus 15:26). What a gift that God chose me for this unique, special-needs adventure. It's stretching me, no doubt. But stretching is what allows us to dig deep into acceptance and freedom.

Clara's life contains little joys, too numerous to count, and I would be a fool to overlook these in the name of unmet expectations.

"So we fix our eyes not on what is seen, but on what is unseen. For what is seen is temporary, but what is unseen is eternal" (2 Corinthians 4:18). So let's fix our eyes. Let's keep fighting for that deep joy hidden beneath layers of hurt and shattered dreams. And let's keep resolving to trust, even if unlike Moses and his people, the waters never part. Because even in the "even if not," our God is still so good, and His promises do not fade. Even if God doesn't open Clara's mouth, even if she never utters a word in my lifetime, even if not … God is still good, and joy still abounds. Because here's the secret to it all …

Victory has already been won! The prize is ours for the taking. Clara's ability to speak is not the prize, the ultimate triumph. It is our access to Jesus that is the prize, and that was gifted to us on the cross. Jesus is it! Not whatever I feel He isn't giving or the prayer I feel He isn't answering. Not Clara's vocal chords … Jesus.

Regardless of our circumstance, we have gained it all. We will never be overtaken by circumstance because Jesus has already overcome! Let's not miss the biggest blessing of all, the gift of Jesus Christ, because we are too zoned in on fleshly circumstance. The desert we face is big, but our God is bigger.

Let's not miss our life because we were expecting a different one.

"While Aaron was speaking to the whole Israelite community, they looked toward the desert, and there was the glory of the Lord appearing in the cloud" (Exodus 16:10).

God's glory still shines in the desert, but we must actively look for it.

It is the broken pieces of our story that God uses to rebuild us into a stronger, more joy-filled version of ourselves. Piece by piece and layer by layer, He breaks us down, but He doesn't leave us there—He rebuilds. He takes the ashes, all the slivered parts, and gives them a new name. He gives close attention to each section, giving each brick personal consideration; He doesn't build blindly.

It is in the rebuilding process that He prepares us for the next obstacle, the next hurt, the next desert encounter, or the next moment of loss. Each brick laid in the building process is a bit stronger than the one before.

I had no way of knowing this at the time, but this was exactly what God was doing through my anorexia, through my infertility, and through my special-needs daughter. It was in the tearing down and reshaping of my whole life, each brick of my past, that He was paving the way for the biggest hurdle of all.

Real Talk: How has God been breaking you down to build you back up? Be vulnerable and consider sharing these thoughts with a family member or close friend.

Action Steps: Journal whatever thoughts come to mind, and then say a prayer, thanking God for being in control of our life's details. Thank Him for the way He carefully considers each brick as He builds our lives and our stories. If you are currently walking the wilderness, thank Him in advance for the promise that you will emerge stronger and that each brick plays a vital role in the shaping process. Thank Him for the growth that you have seen or the growth that will come as a result.

Chapter 9

And Another (Surprise) Baby Makes Five

I looked down at the $1.00 pregnancy test I bought on a whim. (Yes, Dollar Store pregnancy tests are highly accurate. Please do not waste another penny on those fancy tests that cost a million dollars at the grocery store). Two lines. *Two lines.* Seriously, God? I bought the test by chance, not really thinking it would read positive, and it most definitely read positive. A third baby was on the way. *Oh dear Jesus, just hold me. Here we go again.*

Our oldest was only two and a half years, our second not quite eleven months, and another baby was growing in my womb. Being that I was once that girl who was told, "I'm sorry, but there's a chance you won't ever conceive naturally," and, "You most likely will always need medical intervention if you would like more children," this was getting comical. Well, okay then, professional doctors, apparently you have *no clue what you are talking about.* Apparently completing a year and a half of fertility treatments that ended with one successful cycle of in-vitro fertilization is enough to conceive naturally every time my husband looks at me.

I immediately called my sister. She is a schoolteacher, and I typically avoid calling her during work hours. When my number popped up, she knew to answer. "Hey, Britt, what's up?"

My voice was shaking, and my heart was pounding. I blurted out, "I'm pregnant!" A squeal of excitement coupled with a laugh was her reply. I let her know I might or might not be completely losing my cool. Because in approximately eight months, I would have three kids age three and under, and there were already days when I felt stretched to my core and *I didn't even know what to do.*

I called my parents next. They were out shopping; my mom answered, and the first thing from my lips was, "I'm pregnant *again!*"

We laughed, and I cried (tears of happiness and nervousness), and her first question back to me was, "What did Brandon say?" *Oh. Oops.* You mean most wives tell their husbands first when they learn they are expecting half of their man's DNA?

"Well, I haven't actually told him yet." She encouraged me *to maybe hang up and tell my husband.*

I waited to spill the beans until Brandon got home from work. How I made it through this day without losing my mind, I will never know. I found Clara's "Big Sister" shirt and threw it on Camille right as I heard the garage door open.

I sat Camille in her jumper because I knew it would make her cry (just hear me out), and crying could serve as my tactic for getting Brandon to pick her up quickly. Brandon walked in the door, and I faked being super-stressed. "Babe, Camille has been super fussy. Do you mind going to pick her up and hold her for a bit?" And then came the uncontrollable laughter. I couldn't hold it in. I followed behind him, all the while filming and nearly snorting because I knew what was coming.

He looked at me like I had lost my mind. "Why are you filming me?" More laughter. He picked up our crying, almost eleven-month-old baby, and continued to stare back at me, dazed and confused. Then *finally,* he glanced down at her shirt. The next words out of his mouth? And I quote: "You have got to be kidding me."

We announced the pregnancy to extended family and friends

around the twelve-week mark, the safe zone. This is the week where most doctors will tell you the chance of miscarriage is drastically reduced. Our news was met with lots of congratulations and lots of laughs and lots of jokes: *Oops, they did it again!* The days passed, and other than frequent fainting spells on my part (this occurred in my previous pregnancy, but didn't happen quite as early), everything continued normally. We moved forward with typical baby preparations like expecting parents do.

Friends, knowing the size of our house (small), would question, "Will your girls share a room or will you move to a bigger house? Where in the world is this baby going to sleep?" I vividly recall some of the looks to my response: "Oh, the baby will just sleep in our closet. A pack-and-play can fit in there with no problem." Nine times out of ten, said friend would laugh as if I was joking, only to realize I was not joking at all. #thirdchildproblems

The days rolled on, and we continued to plan our epic closet nursery. All the while, I couldn't shake this gut feeling that something was a little off. Something didn't feel right. This was not rooted in worry or fear. No, it was just a momma's deep intuition that there was something different about this pregnancy, this baby. A gut feeling that the wilderness walk was not quite over. I couldn't put my finger on it, but every once in a while, I would mention it to Brandon—not to scare him in any way, but as a way to process what I felt was the Holy Spirit prepping me, prepping us, for something big. I just didn't know what that something was yet.

Whispers of the Spirit

"But when he, the Spirit of truth, comes, he will guide you into all truth. He will not speak on his own, he will speak only what he hears, and he will tell you what is yet to come. He will bring glory to me by taking from what is mine and making it known to you" (John 16:12–15).

When pregnant with Camille, our second child, people

frequently asked if I was worried or fearful that she too would have Cohen Syndrome. Given our 25 percent chance of passing on the double mutation, I can see why this was a common question from outsiders. I can say, with 100 percent certainty, that I was never once concerned with Camille's development. Not once. It was as if God blanketed me with a peace that passes all understanding (Philippians 4:7) and protected me from mental anguish.

From the moment I learned of her existence, to her robust movements in the womb, to the first second her eyes met mine, I never questioned. My mind was steadfast, and a deep peace ran through my bones. It was a non-issue. It was as if God was whispering to me through His Spirit a sense of calmness and immovable security.

This time was different. While I did not live day-to-day in fear of the future—and I still felt peace believing that His ways are perfect—I did not have the same peace, the same resolve, that this baby, our third child, would be completely healthy. What I later realized was that, along with the unsettled feeling in my heart, God had been slowly prepping me behind the scenes for the event to come.

After recovering from anorexia, and while undergoing treatments for infertility, I started a blog to document our story, my testimony, and the Lord's work in our lives. Writing has always been a therapeutic outlet for me, so I figured pressing into this up-and-coming resource would be an all-too-easy way to shine a little bit of Jesus into a small space of the internet.

Somewhere along the way, my path crossed with Maria Furlough, author of the blog *True Worth* (mytrueworth.org). I was drawn to Maria's blog because her message was simple: our true worth is soul-deep, not skin-deep, and comes from an identity in Jesus, not an identity in the world. Her words were so powerful and her writing convicting that I continued to follow her blog over the years.

In 2013, pregnant with her third child, she learned that the baby in her womb would most likely not live long on this earth due to a condition called Potter's Syndrome. On March 31, 2014, her son Gideon was born breathing, but on this day he also took his last breath. I continued to follow Maria's writings after Gideon's death and remember the way she balanced, and continues to balance, grief and pain with hope and joy. I was awestruck by her deep faith in the midst of such a deep loss and inspired by the way she resolved to tell of God's goodness despite a circumstance that felt far from good.

Several months after Gideon's passing, Maria held a giveaway on her blog to pass on two blue bracelets with the words *"Gideon Strong,* My peace I give you," and a painting her mother created titled *Shades of Peace.* Both represented what this family had come to experience on a deep level ... that because of Jesus, there is overflowing abundance and unwavering peace, even in our darkest moments. I commented on that post with the following:

"Your story has touched many. I have been so blessed by your transparent reflections. It is amazing how God can use such pain and heartache and turn it into good, and dare I say ... even joy? My oldest daughter, now age two, has some severe developmental delays. We learned back in November 2013 that she has Cohen Syndrome (confirmed via genetic testing). Your story has reminded me that God is so very *good.* All the time. No matter what. And that *joy* can be found even in the midst of confusion and pain. Even in the midst of death (to me this means death of the type of child I envisioned when dreaming of growing our family). Thank you for your encouragement and allowing Gideon to make a difference."

I think it no coincidence that the bracelets and painting sit on Clara's bookshelf as a reminder that God is good all the time and that joy abounds even in the middle of life's disappointments, even in the midst of our desert walks.

As the months passed, our friendship flourished, and to this day Maria and I read each other's blogs and share encouragement via e-mail messages. At the time of the giveaway, I assumed the message was relating to my experience with Clara, but little did I know, as

2014 turned into 2015, the foreshadowing the Lord was gracing me with bit by little bit.

It was near the time I won that giveaway that God prompted me to read Angie Smith's *I Will Carry You*. This was an odd choice for leisurely reading, as the subject matter is heavy and centered on child loss, but I clearly heard God telling me to get my hands on a copy. A few clicks and a two-day delivery guarantee later, the book was on its way. I threw myself into the pages and got swept away in her story. A pregnancy, a surprising diagnosis, and a heartbreaking experience of holding her child as she breathed her last breath ... this was the premise of Angie's testimony. I finished the last page and pondered, *This was so gut-wrenchingly hard and beautiful, yet why in the world did you want me to read this, Lord? Because surely this is an experience far too distant from any reality of mine.*

As I sat in awe of our third pregnancy, this new baby on the way, my mind was continually drawn back to Maria and Angie and their stories. The feeling that this pregnancy was different continued to be strong. I still wasn't sure what God was prepping me for, but I didn't assume death was in our future. I assumed the Spirit's whispers were a way to prepare my heart and mind for another Cohen's baby, or a different condition or syndrome altogether. I wrestled with these feelings as the pregnancy continued, not out of fear, but as a way to prepare.

Yet a mother is never prepared for what might be the deepest loss of all, the loss of her child.

> Real Talk: Have you ever felt the Holy Spirit's whisper? If so, think about this time in your life and reflect on how God used His Spirit to prepare your heart for a certain life event.
>
> Action Steps: Ask God to make alive His Spirit inside of you. Maybe you have never experienced this power, or maybe you are desperate for more. Ask that the Spirit dwell and make His home in your heart so you can experience more of this incredible gift.

April Fools, but This Was No Joke

April 1, 2015 arrived. April Fool's Day. We were eager for 1:00 p.m. to roll around because it was then that we would learn the sex of our third baby. Anatomy scan day was always my favorite day during pregnancy. There is something so sacred, so holy, about lying there as the technician scans your baby from head to toe, a baby who is wiggling away and whose heart is pumping to the beat of a drum. It's a worship experience of sorts: Praising God for who He is, the Creator of life, and thanking Him for blessing you with this miracle. Because any baby in the womb is a miracle, regardless of how long one yearned for it to be there.

My bet was pink and Brandon's blue, and we joked about what life would be like with three females (hello, teenage years!) or with one little male who had to endure life with two older sisters (hello, teenage years!). We arrived eager to see our baby and to share the good news with family and friends. The technician seemed equally eager and, after learning we had two girls at home, commented on how fun it was going to be to surprise us in a few moments with the news.

Yet, right when she started the scan, I knew something wasn't right. My eyes flashed across the screen, looking for the heartbeat, and I couldn't find it.

The technician ever so gently started in with her questions …

"When did you say your last ultrasound was?" At ten weeks' gestation.

"Okay, and when did you see your doctor last?" Two weeks ago, eighteen weeks and three days pregnant. Everything looked great at that appointment. Heartbeat was in the one-fifties.

"Are you still feeling some pregnancy symptoms?" Yes.

"Okay. I'm just taking a few quick measurements, and then I'm going to have the doctor come in."

Quick measurements? I wondered. Anatomy scans are detailed and lengthy—quick is not an adjective I would ever use. And with that, I knew my initial observation was correct. I asked if there was a heartbeat, to which she replied she was not finding one, she was so sorry, and she would page the doctor immediately to come in and meet with us.

I stared up at the television screen, hoping this was a mistake. But my baby wasn't moving—just lying there, peaceful yet lifeless.

Time stood still. All I could do was release my tears. I was dreaming the worst nightmare imaginable, yet I was unable to wake up. The doctor, a high-risk specialist, came in and appropriately but compassionately explained that, based on the images she was seeing, our baby had died and there was no immediate reason or explainable cause for the death (no concern with the spine or brain). She explained some potential causes for a second trimester loss, the testing options available if we were interested in investigating the cause of death, and our options moving forward for delivery of the child.

Delivery of my dead baby.

This, Lord? This is what you have gently been preparing me for over the last five months? Death? This was the reason for the gut feeling and the Holy Spirit whispers?

Dear Jesus, how am I supposed to deliver a child that I don't get to take home? How am I supposed to push a baby out of my body who isn't breathing? Whose cries I will never hear? Whose eyes will never meet mine? This can't be happening, Lord! I am not cut out for this. I am not this strong. Lord, I am not ready for this type of pain, this wilderness walk, this dark, isolating journey that lies ahead. I can't do this. Haven't we been through enough? An hour ago, my tambourine was raised, and now you're throwing me back into the wilderness, just like the Israelites. Why bless us with this miracle only to take it away twenty weeks later? Jesus, show up, because I can hardly breathe.

Within minutes, our parents were informed and my mom was by our side. We were eventually moved into a private counseling room to talk further with the doctor and a genetics counselor. My demeanor was to the point, all black and white: *Please give me the hard facts so I can get out of here.* Brandon was glazed, face white as snow. He hardly spoke a word. We left several hours later, and we felt like we were walking into a deep fog. The air so thick that we could hardly push through to take the next step.

We sat in our car and cried and hardly moved. "What are we supposed to do right now? Do we keep sitting here? Do we go home? Is this really happening?" I kept asking Brandon on repeat. Within a matter of seconds, our world went from light and carefree to heavy and burdensome. We went home and crawled in bed and just held each other. Because truly ... what are you supposed to do in these moments? I couldn't eat and couldn't sleep because how do you eat or sleep when you know the baby in your womb, who was alive just days before, is no longer breathing? What are you supposed to do when your world comes crashing down? Nothing feels good or right or normal in these moments.

The news spread, and within a few hours, dinner was delivered to our door. Another family showed up with cookies and ice cream, a card, and, best of all, open arms. No words or faith-based explanations as to why this came to be, just an embrace that said it all. I don't think I've ever cried that hard in the presence of my friends, but I'm so thankful they showed up. Meals continued to be organized and prayers lifted on our behalf.

My doctor was out of town the day we got the news but called us as soon as the hospital got in touch with him. We had several options for delivery: Wait a week or so until my body went into labor naturally, thus making the delivery process much quicker, or be admitted to the hospital for induction, knowing that it could take twenty-four to forty-eight hours for my body to birth the baby. Both scenarios allowed my doctor to deliver and allowed us time with the baby post-birth.

A final option was a dilation and evacuation (D&E), yet this procedure would be performed by a doctor I didn't know, in a small sterile room in a different hospital, would take approximately thirty minutes, and I would not be allowed to see or hold the baby.

Each option held pros and cons and potential for trauma, but traditional delivery of my baby seemed the most appropriate option for me and my healing. For Brandon's healing. But I couldn't wait for my body to recognize the loss. I needed to induce as soon as my doctor returned. I couldn't fathom walking around day after day after day, knowing that my child was dead. I couldn't fathom walking around wondering if today was the day my body would go into labor. I couldn't bear the public's questioning of my pregnancy. And I needed to see my baby, hold him or her in my arms, and have the traditional hospital experience. Yet, there is nothing traditional about birthing a child who is already walking the streets of heaven.

Arrangements were made, and we were scheduled to start the induction at midnight on April 4, 2015. At 11:22 p.m. on April 3, several minutes before we walked out the door to the hospital, I published the following post on my blog:

This is the hardest post I have ever had to write …

Some of you know that this past Wednesday, April 1ˢᵗ, our world came crashing down. Totally unexpected. No warning signs. No hints that this particular appointment would be any different.

We were scheduled for our 20-week anatomy scan this past Wednesday and arrived eager and thrilled to see our baby and learn if we were expecting another precious girl or an adorable little boy. The technician seemed equally as eager and, after learning we had two girls at home, commented on how fun it was going to be to surprise us in a few moments with the news.

Yet right when she started the scan, I knew something wasn't right. My eyes were flashing across the screen looking for the heartbeat, and I couldn't find it …

We are so overwhelmed with the love and kindness that has been shown to us over the last 48 hours. Phone calls, texts, surprise gifts and food drop offs, scripture reminders … everything. We certainly do feel the love and support from our family and friends.

We will be admitted to the hospital shortly to start the induction and delivery process. The doctor explained it could take 1-2 days. We are so thankful that we will be given the option of seeing and holding the baby if we so choose.

This is by far the hardest thing we have ever had to do. All we know to do is pray for strength and pray that God alone would be glorified by our experience and story. While we would not wish this experience on anyone, we are thankful for the reminder that on this Easter weekend, death does not have the final say. Not then. Not now. Not ever. In the coming hours we will hold our precious baby, who is already being held in the arms of Jesus. And we will put our hope in Him alone and in the promise of seeing our little one again on the other side.

I think it no coincidence that we were admitted to the hospital on Good Friday, the day that Jesus willingly died to free us from our sin and give us an abundance of hope despite life's hurts, despite our many wilderness moments. The reality that Jesus died to take away death was the message I hung to as we silently rode the elevator to the labor and delivery unit. While I would hold death in my arms in just a few hours, the Spirit gently reminded me that death isn't the end of the story. Death makes way for life, for new growth, for fresh hope and joy.

Death doesn't win because Jesus already won. Life doesn't end with death; death, for a believer, is the richest beginning of all.

Brandon and I didn't talk much as we entered the hospital. Small talk felt odd given the circumstance. My hands were shaking and my heart pounding as we arrived at the front desk. I gave them my name, and the nurse's eyes met mine as she perfectly yet ever so quietly conveyed her condolences. The chatter at their station silenced, I assume out of respect for our situation. Hugs were exchanged, and we were shown to Room 307, a room forever be etched in my memory.

I didn't want to enter that room. Not one ounce of me wanted to walk through those doors, despite it being the biggest and nicest room on the floor, because the next time I walked through them, my child would no longer be with me. I wanted to turn and run and hide. I wanted to delay the inevitable. But as I entered Room 307, God gently gave me Deuteronomy 31:6 on which to meditate: "Be strong and courageous. Do not be afraid or terrified … for the Lord your God goes with you; he will never leave you or forsake you."

Be strong.

Don't be afraid.

God will meet me in this very room.

He's not going anywhere.

He doesn't expect me to fight alone.

This desert land is suffocating, but joy wins.

Because Jesus already won.

<u>Real Talk:</u> Has there been a time in your life when you wanted to run away, run from the open door God was asking you to walk through? What in your life feels like your own Room 307?

<u>Action Steps:</u> Ask God to give you the courage to walk through the door in trust, whatever it is. Acknowledge your feelings and your reservations and your hurts, but ask for trust and peace and praise to shine brighter than your feelings. Then take His hand and take that first step.

Chapter 10

The Silent Delivery Room

April 3, 2015

1:50 p.m.: We enter Room 307, the master suite, and meet my night nurse, Ms. Priscilla. She is sweet and considerate and also forthcoming on how this event might take place, all the ways this birth could *actually* happen. She explains that since the baby is so small and since an epidural is a must, given the amount of meds they will give me, women sometimes do not feel the pressure to push as the baby comes down and suddenly realize the baby has been born and is sitting between their legs. *Dear God, please don't let it happen this way, please.* I text family and friends to please pray that this not be our scenario. Priscilla explains that sometimes the induction and delivery can take up to forty-eight hours, but sometimes a woman responds much more quickly and the baby is born within hours. We have no way of knowing. Priscilla shares that we will get a memory box for the baby, and they will attempt to get feet and hand prints.

April 4, 2015

12:24 a.m.: My dad, mom, older sister, and sister-in-law arrive to sit with us for a while. (My younger sister was sweet enough to stay home with our nephews and niece, and my brother stayed home with his newborn twins. Brandon's family would be in first thing in the morning.) Originally, I had stated we would just "sleep" and didn't need anyone at the hospital those first few hours. Goodness, I am so thankful God smacked me over the head on that one. We needed those bodies there that night. I ask Priscilla to please check one more time that my baby's heartbeat is gone before starting the medication. She checks. The Doppler is silent. Tears burst from my eyes. She asks if I am ready to continue. No, but I have no other choice.

Blood work begins, and I get queasy, per usual. I hate that initial IV. Like, if I had to rate it on a scale of favorite part to least favorite part on the birth experience scale, it would fall under least favorite. Stick a needle in my back any day, but please don't stick my arm. Priscilla tells me she gets queasy administering IVs when her patients get queasy during IVs, so basically we are a winning combination. I ask a lot of questions about the birth and after birth, how much time we will be allowed with the baby, if my milk will come in, etc. I need the facts so I can mentally prepare.

1:32 a.m.: I spike a fever. At some point, Priscilla begins my induction medication. She explains that for a typical full-term induction, patients are given 24 ml of medicine every four hours, but in my case, I will be given 600 ml every six hours. Well, okay then. She explains that when the contractions begin, they will come on fast and strong. This is necessary, though, to force my body into delivery mode.

3:01 a.m.: I start to feel cramping, and my hips become tight. Brandon leaves to use the restroom and notices a photo of a white rose on the door to our room. The rose symbolizes pregnancy loss and serves as a sign to let the hospital staff and others know to be sensitive when entering.

3:50 a.m.: My parents, sister, and sister-in-law leave to catch some sleep. We ask them to please leave their cell phone ringers on full volume should we need them. My dad prays over us and our baby before leaving. Brandon and I try to close our eyes and sleep, but how does one sleep knowing the events to come?

6:20 a.m.: Priscilla comes in to check on us and explains I will meet my new nurse at 7 a.m., at shift change. I am given more meds. Brandon and I joke that the toilet in our room has the world's longest flush. Seriously, it would flush for a solid minute. And it was loud enough to wake up the entire L&D floor. So that was really special. It became a joke anytime someone would use our restroom.

7:00 a.m.: Nurse Reena comes in and introduces herself. She will be my nurse for the day, and most likely for the delivery of the baby. She asks me how I feel about an epidural. I explain I can wait a while longer as I am not in too much pain. Reena states that I don't want to wait too long because the pain level will increase rapidly once it begins. She reminds me gently that, since I will be working through severe emotional pain, I don't need to experience any physical pain. Reena is a smart woman. Reena explains that anytime I need to cry or vent or scream, she will sit with me for as long as I need. She offers to pray with us at any time. Reena is our angel dressed in scrubs.

7:19 a.m.: Contractions coming every two minutes; Reena and Dr. G. decide to hold off on more medicine. We don't want the contractions coming on too strong and fast, as rupturing the incision site of my previous C-section is a real risk.

7:30 a.m.: Reena runs through a long list of questions regarding my history. She also gives us some facts about deceased babies, birth weight requirements for burial, etc. She also shares information about funeral home options and pregnancy-loss support groups.

8:50 a.m.: The epidural is complete, and Dr. G comes in to see us. He has us sign the forms to consent to genetic testing, to investigate the cause of death. We cried when Dr. G walked in. This sweet man has delivered my two living babies, and now he is delivering my one deceased baby. All the memories flash before my eyes in that moment. Clara's birth, Camille's birth, and now this … a stillbirth.

It is sometime in the nine o'clock hour that our family arrives back at the hospital.

10:15 a.m.: A sweet friend, Sharon—and ironically Dr. G's wife—shows up to be with us for the day. She has done this for all of my deliveries. Another sweet friend, Tiffany, shows up to capture our day in pictures. Words cannot express how thankful I am to have these women with me, both as a distraction but also as an anchor of support. What a witness of selfless love.

11:34 a.m.: I try to nap as the lack of sleep from the night before is catching up to me. I nap off and on for a few minutes.

12:00 p.m.: Reena comes in to check me and also puts in a catheter. Everyone is laughing at how much urine I had been holding. Reena states this is the most urine she has ever seen! I explain, "This is what happens when y'all crazy people give me approximately fifty bags of liquids via IV." We all get a good laugh.

I ask Tiffany to take some photographs of us with all sides of the family. I want pictures of smiles and laughter and hope because the photographs to come will be more pain and tear-filled.

Reena comes to check me again. I am making progress and am not to have any more medicine until 6:00 p.m. Reena thinks the baby will arrive before 6:00 p.m. *Oh Jesus, we are getting closer. Please, God, just come quickly. I am not sure I am up for this task, this assignment You have placed in my lap.* Reena comments on my strength. Sweet Reena, if you see any strength, it is because God is supernaturally infusing me; it is not of myself. Without my God holding me, I would crumble.

2:40 p.m.: Reena comes back in to check me, and I'm now dilated to 3 cm. I only have to get to 5 or 6 since the baby is so small. Reena says she can feel the baby. I am feeling more pressure, and the pain is coming on again strong. Family and Sharon encourage me to get more anesthesia. I hesitate because, while the pain is strong, I don't want Priscilla's warning to be my reality. *I don't want my baby to just fall out.* I can't handle this pain, but I want to be aware enough to know when the birth is happening. The anesthesiologist comes in to check and gives me a fresh dose of meds, per my consent. I pray for just enough relief, but not too much.

Reena presents to me a card signed by the entire nursing staff. I cry because, goodness, what a gift. To read their encouragement in that moment—priceless.

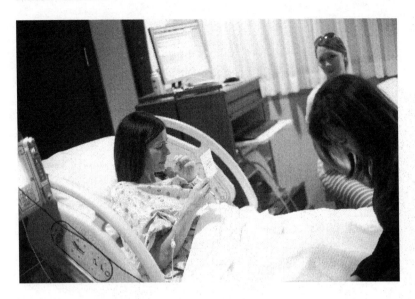

3:00 p.m.: Reena comes back in to check on me … I am making progress, and I am also much happier now that the pain has subsided. Reena states we are getting close to meeting our baby.

I ask Reena to check me again. I am feeling pressure.

4:30 p.m.: Our parents, siblings, Sharon, Tiffany, and Reena come in to pray over us. Emotions flow free. I don't want the prayer to end because I know what awaits me on the other side. The prayer ends, and Dr. G arrives shortly after. I have to catch my breath because *the time has come. I will soon meet my baby, who has already met Jesus.*

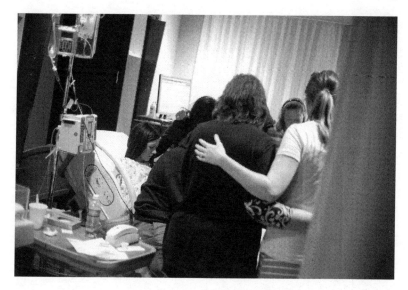

The men of the family leave the room, Brandon included. Brandon and I had agreed that he should do what he felt capable of doing, in that moment. There would be no hurt feelings or regrets or guilt. We kiss good-bye, not knowing when we might see each other again, as he is undecided if he wants to meet our baby. I pray boldly for God to open wide his heart. The women of the family stay by my side. I need bodies in this room. I need faces to meet mine.

Dr. G and the nurses take a seat on the sofa next to my hospital bed. Less than a minute passes, and I ask them to check me; I can feel pressure. Dr. G states it's time. And it is here that time almost stands still, like I am in a dream. The preparations, the overhead lights, the team that swarms in … it is all the same. The same things happen whether the baby is alive or dead. The nurse asks me to give one practice push. They think the baby will arrive with one or two more pushes. I push again; the nurse counts for me. I let out a loud cry: "This hurts so bad!" I then explain that I hurt emotionally, not physically. Brandon later tells me he heard my cries and assumed I was in physical pain. Dr. G asks me to push once more, no counting this time, and within seconds, I feel my baby being born. *Thank you, Jesus, for this answered prayer.*

4:49 p.m.: Our third child enters the world. The room is silent. There is no noise, only hushed commotion—no cries from my babe. The air is thick, but peace is present. I look up and ask my sister, "Does my baby look like a baby?"

"Oh goodness, yes," she replies.

I then ask, "Is it a boy or a girl?"

All goes quiet for several seconds, and Dr. G gently replies, "It's a boy." Brandon lets out a cry from the sitting room.

The nurses gently clean off my son. They weigh and measure him. 6.6 ounces and 7 inches of perfection. They wrap him in a tiny blanket and place a tiny hat on his head. He is little, yet amazingly formed. The nurse brings him over to me to see for the first time. She encourages me: "Remember him like this, Mom. His body will change rapidly. Remember him like this."

She asks if I want to hold him. She has already cautioned the family to be careful, as his body is quite delicate and he could easily slip out of the blanket that holds him. I can't risk that happening. I want to hold him, but will wait until I'm able to sit up.

Nurse Reena very loudly exclaims, "Now it's time for your cute panties!" Thank you, Nurse Reena, for the comic relief. Anyone who has birthed a baby knows that the hospital underwear, which they so graciously gift you, can be described as anything but cute. We all get a good laugh.

The next thing I know, Brandon appears from behind the curtain. He meets his son. We cry and smile and cry and smile some more. The pain is real, but joy abounds. *Thank you, Jesus, for this answered prayer. Thank you for nudging my husband to come in, to come in and meet our third child.*

We name him Chance Michael. Chance is my biological mom's maiden name. My mom is with Jesus, so passing on her name to our son, who also resides in heaven, just seems to fit. Michael is Brandon's middle name.

I eventually hold him. The second I look at his face, a deep peace rushes through my body. I feel this deep peace every time I take in his tiny features. His nose is by far the cutest nose I have ever seen. Everyone is commenting on his nose. Every detail of his body is perfectly identifiable. It is breathtaking to hold such a tiny, complete being in your arms. I want to take in every second. I want time to stop in Room 307 because if I could just stop time, my son would always be with me. His body wouldn't start to decompose. This moment wouldn't come to pass. His mouth is open, and I gently press it closed with my fingers. The sting of death is less obvious when his mouth is closed. I stroke his cheeks ever so softly and rub the yellow hat that sits gently on his head.

I have a son, I keep repeating in my mind. *God, I don't know why we are walking this road, why you gifted us with a son only to take him away, but I'm choosing to trust because you've not let me down before.*

My trust does not take away the incredible sense of pain I feel, but I will praise you through the pain. Give me your strength, Father, because the hours ahead, the inevitable, the saying good-bye, might literally rip my heart from my chest.

Family members hold Chance and spend time admiring his cute-as-a-button nose. They comment on his features. Tears are shed, but so are smiles and laughter. God gifts us with what feels like a celebration, despite deep hurt. It's a celebration of His love and faithfulness and peace, despite great loss, despite holding death in our arms. Death was present in our very room, but with this death came the reminder of the sweet afterlife. Heaven never felt closer than when cradling a life already living there.

Oh Jesus, come quickly. Let's all go home.

7:00 p.m.: Reena comes to say her good-byes. She prays and give hugs and says, "You are the strongest mom I know," and I remind her, "No, I don't act out of my own strength. It is God in this place. Thank you for playing your part in our story." Reena introduces me to my new nurse, who will be the one to walk Chance out of the room in a few short hours, and who will tend to us during the night.

As the hours pass, the room starts to clear. I order pizza from the cafeteria, not because I feel like eating but because I must do the next normal thing. And the next normal thing when your stomach is growling is to eat. If I am going to walk out of this room tomorrow and chose life over despair, I must do the next normal thing, now. The pizza is half-baked, and since I can't stomach the thought of eating soggy pizza dough, my dad orders pizza to be delivered. I pass Chance off to my sister. I eat. I go through the motions. The hunger pangs are relieved, but the heart pangs remain.

Our siblings leave. They have been dear enough to stay with us all day. Our parents stay and continue the job of securing a funeral home. They have been working on this all day, bless them. Apparently, funeral homes aren't quick to respond on the weekend. Go figure—as if death reserves itself for the business week. It was a job we just couldn't take on, because how could we call to secure pick-up and transport of our dead baby when our dead baby was still in my womb? Emotions were too high for this task, and our parents graciously, without complaint, took it on. We are forever grateful.

As the parents continue phone calls in the hallway, Brandon and I are left alone with Chance. We talk some, but also sit in silence to take in these last moments. The clock is ticking fast, but we don't want to speak of it.

Chance has been with us for five hours, and we agree that it is time. His body is changing quickly now, and we want to preserve his memory in our minds.

10:00 p.m.: We call the nurse to let her know we are ready. Except I wasn't really. How is anyone ready for such a moment? Our mothers come in to say good-bye to their grandson and to support us in that heart-wrenching moment. I kiss my son's head once last time, as does Brandon, and I ever so slowly pass him off to the nurse. She gently unwraps Chance from the blanket and removes his hat, and I let out a cry: "Oh, baby, I love you so much." The nurse carries him to the warming bed, places him in, and sweetly sings to him as she wheels him out of the room.

And just like that, my son is gone. The child I birthed from my body five hours earlier is now gone, for good. Of all the moments in Room 307, this is by far the worst. We are left sitting in our sadness, with no baby to fill our arms. The room is eerily quiet, just as it was when Chance entered the world. Night has fallen, and I dread the hours ahead because, despite deep emotional and physical exhaustion, somehow I must force my eyes to close and my mind to settle. Peace was present, but so was pain. Hours of darkness lie ahead, and I must fight for the light of day.

11:30 p.m.: Brandon calls the funeral home to confirm they have safely picked up our son from the hospital. They have. Our nurse also confirms. We had to know, had to be sure, before attempting rest.

April 5, 2015

6:00 a.m.: My eyes open as my nurse places the blood pressure cuff on my arm. She's here to take my vitals. She hadn't bothered us in the night, bless her. She tells me later that she knew my body needed the rest, in more ways than one. By the grace of God, we slept six hours. Unlike my other birth experiences, I am able to move around more freely, with less pain. Another answered prayer.

I continue to see bits of His goodness even in the midst of our tragedy. I must focus my mind here, for there is always goodness to be found. Even in death, His goodness remains. This is where I must settle my mind in the days ahead because the hardest days are yet to come.

My nurse explains the shift change is coming, and she will be leaving at 7:00 a.m. I thank her for her kindness, gentleness, and encouragement, and let her know that her song to Chance will always be remembered.

It's Easter Sunday, the day we celebrate the Lord's resurrection. The day we celebrate that Jesus's death wasn't the end of the story—it was just the beginning. The irony isn't lost on me. As the sun rises that morning outside the window of Room 307, hope also rises. Because life doesn't really end with death. My only son isn't lying lonely in a morgue; he is breathing and singing and walking along the streets of heaven. That's beauty right there. That's hope. That's joy. I still ache with sadness because I am simply a mommy who misses her boy (this perhaps will always be my story), but the sadness doesn't overcome. Because Jesus already did.

9:00 a.m.: Friends stop by to hug our necks and to sit with us for a while. The fact that they took time, on their Easter Sunday, to sit at our feet and share in Chance's story? I am forever grateful. We share about Chance's birth and what we will forever remember about him. We share the good parts, the funny parts, and the hard parts. All of it—because it is all a part of Chance's story, God's story. They gift us with a beautiful blue blanket with Chance's full name and birthdate embroidered on the front.

12:00 p.m.: Nurse Paula explains that, since there are no concerns with my vitals or healing, I am free to be discharged. I am told to see Dr. G in two weeks—for both a physical and emotional postpartum well check. I am given prescriptions to fill and a Rhogam shot due to my Rh-negative status. (I cannot tell you how many Rhogam shots I have had during pregnancy or post-delivery ... it is getting comical.) Brandon's parents arrive to help see us out, and they load our car. Nurse Paula reviews my discharge summary, but keeps it brief given the situation. She retrieves a wheelchair and lets me know, if I'm ready, she can wheel me downstairs.

My eyes meet many as I am wheeled through the labor and delivery floor. Family members of other expecting patients look away as they quickly realize my arms are empty. There is no car seat or diaper bag or miscellaneous accessories. Just us and the wheelchair.

As we approach the nurses station before exiting the floor, I see two beautiful faces: the cleaning lady who, every time she attended to my room would stop and smile and give me a hug, and a nurse who helped assist in Chance's birth, the one who was on my left and counted as I pushed. They stop and cry and hug me so intently I can still feel it.

Brandon pulls the car around, and Nurse Paula helps me out of the wheelchair. We say our good-byes. She hugs me and cries and assures us that she will be in prayer for our strength and healing. I am so grateful for the prayers, for I know I will need them.

And just like that, it's over. I watch the other cars on our drive home and am astounded that the rest of the world is simply moving as normal. People are smiling and laughing and living their life, and *how in the world am I supposed to do that?* My son is gone. My baby boy was in my womb and now he is not and, goodness, it would be nice if God could just freeze time, just stop the hustle and bustle of the world until I am on the other side of this grief journey.

But the world keeps moving, and so must I.

Chapter 11

Build Your House

I remember the moment like it was yesterday. There I stood, in the middle of a graveyard, heart pounding, head spinning, and literally no words on my tongue. *How did I get here? What am I doing here? Is this all really happening?* These questions were plastered on my pale face as we walked from plot to plot to plot, attempting to pick the perfect resting spot for our son. Our son. Our son who was born still two days prior, twenty weeks too early. How could this be? While my physical body was present, mentally I was far away. The cemetery director talked us through our options, and Brandon occasionally turned and asked, "What do you think, babe?"

What do I think?

I think I wasn't prepared for this. I think this all happened too fast. I think I want to go back and freeze time to the moment our son was in my arms and I could touch his little face and stare at his perfect nose. That is what I think.

"I don't know, babe," I replied. "I can't even fathom making this decision. I feel like I'm going to burst. I have no idea. I trust you. Can you please just decide for us? Please?"

And in that moment of wanting to freeze time, I heard very

clearly the Lord whispering to me, "But you were prepared for this. Your faith in the One who does not change is what will pull you through. I will pull you through. Your hope in life after death is what will keep moving you forward. You were prepared for this because you spent time tending your soil and building your house."

God graciously brought to mind His teachings in Matthew chapter 7. Jesus encourages His followers to be wise and to build their houses on rock, the one and only true, solid foundation, so that when the storms of life come, when the desert walks come, the houses will not fall. Jesus compares a house built on rock to one built on sand. And we all know how well sand withstands a storm, be it water or wind. Not well. When the winds pick up, the sand is scattered and tossed and thrown with vengeance. Scattered. Tossed. Thrown. Sand cannot stand up to the trials this life throws our way. It was never intended to. God did not create sand for the mighty task of house support.

> Therefore everyone who hears these words of mine and puts them into practice is like a wise man who built his house on the rock. The rain came down, the streams rose, and the winds blew and beat against that house; *yet it did not fall,* because it had its foundation on the rock. But everyone who hears these words of mine and does not put them into practice is like a foolish man who built his house on the sand. The rain came down, the streams rose, and the winds blew and beat against that house, *and it fell with a great crash.* (Matthew 7: 24–27, emphasis added)

Since losing Chance, the truth of Matthew 7 has become so real and so alive to me. Here is what I am being reminded of and what keeps me moving forward, day after day, pursuing the Creator of the universe. Even on days when I don't feel like it. Even on days when I want to give in and cave. Even on days when I'm walking the cemetery.

When crisis hits, we don't have time to build our foundation.

The foundation must already be laid. We must put in the work upfront so that when the dark clouds come rolling in, *and they will*, we will not be thrown under. We must *invest daily* in foundation work. Yes, we might be taken by surprise, but our foundation won't. Foundation work is what gives us the assurance during the storm, during the wait, during the yuck that our tambourine dance is just around the corner. So how do we invest daily, to create this rock infrastructure described in Matthew 7?

<u>Intentionality.</u> This is what I have learned: I have to get to the place of making intentional choices, day after day after day. Spending time in the Word, reading it for what it is, and asking God to help me understand the words on the page is key. I cannot claim the promises of Scripture, promises that hold me up when the desert walk comes, if I do not know them. Spending time in prayer is a second key component. Prayer builds on the truth of Scripture. The act of prayer is intentional worship: talking to Him, claiming His truths, thanking Him for His sovereignty, wrestling through my struggles and areas of sin and pride. Prayer might feel odd at first—it did for me—but over time, it becomes a more natural way of living.

I want to practice worshipping Him through prayer in the good times so that this same worship naturally flows from my lips in the bad times.

Intentionality might take some sacrifice of time or schedule or even sleep. Building with sand is a much easier option. But let's think of the tradeoff here. Am I trading rock for sand in my daily choices of making Christ an intentional part of my day?

<u>Stillness.</u> In our current generational mindset, being still is not a popular life choice. We are inundated with constant to-dos and enough social media options to keep us constantly moving from one thing to the next to the next. Noise is not lacking in our generation, and intentional stillness is not seen as a virtue but a character flaw.

But what I have come to find is that sometimes it is necessary to shut it all down. To rest before our Creator with hearts and hands wide open. To be completely still before the Lord and just sit and listen. To say, "Okay, I am here with no agenda and no 'please make this happen for me or my family' list. I am ready to receive what you have for me, so please speak so that I can hear you."

Learning to be still in the times of plenty helps us hear His voice so much more clearly when famine strikes, when we are left in the desert with no manna in sight.

Stillness produces mental clarity. And we so need this mental clarity when walking through the graveyard of loss or financial crisis or family disappointment or medical diagnosis (or whatever has you wandering the desert).

We left the cemetery that day, and while I still felt a sense of overwhelm, I knew the overwhelm would not overcome. I had a choice to make: I could choose to place my hope in my ever-changing emotions, or I could choose to place my hope in the rock on which our home was built. Investing in foundation work is investing in faith, and investing in faith is investing in the hope that will pull us through when the waves creep in and threaten to throw us overboard.

Let's invest.

Let's be intentional.

Let's be still.

Let's build our house.

Chapter 12

Blue Balloons

We celebrated Chance's short life with a graveside service on April 7, 2015. We had a vision for this moment, and our family and friends delivered. It was our desire that the feel of the morning point to life, not death, so we requested that everyone dress causal and comfortable, in bright colors, and for families to please bring their young children. I didn't think I could handle a bunch of people showing up in black suits and ties. That just sets the tone for seriousness and sadness. I needed normalcy, so I needed color and I needed the children of our world roaming the cemetery.

We also asked that each family bring several blue balloons to be released at the end of the service, in honor of our son and as a visual reminder that, just as the balloons fly up to the heavens, that is where our son was flying now, too. That heaven is real and alive and what this life is all about.

I am reminded of the omer of manna that the Israelites saved, to serve as visual reminder of God's faithfulness. A jar of the heavenly bread was set aside in hopes that when joy started to fade and grumbling returned, the people could look back and remember God's perfect provision. So that others, in future generations, would also remember God's provision and care. In a way, the blue balloons served as my jar of manna.

> The people of Israel called the bread manna. It was white like coriander seed and tasted like wafers made with honey. Moses said, "This is what the Lord has commanded: "Take an omer of manna and keep it for the generations to come, so they can see the bread I gave you to eat in the desert when I brought you out of Egypt." So Moses said to Aaron, "Take a jar and put an omer of manna in it. Then place it before the Lord to be kept for the generations to come." (Exodus 16:31–33)

As I made my way to the front of the open-air pavilion, hugging and greeting people along the way, Chance's casket caught my eye. It took my breath away because caskets should never be that small. Our parents had picked out his casket and the tiny arrangement of flowers that sat on top. It was perfect and everything I would have chosen. I just didn't have the strength to choose these things myself. Part of me wanted to rip off the top so I could scoop my son up again, as if I could delay his being buried in the ground. I noticed out of the corner of my eye a small tree at the front of the open-air pavilion. In the base of the tree sat a blue picture frame with a sketched image of a tree, the word *Loved* underneath, and a blue birdhouse that hung from the branches. "That tree!" I exclaimed.

"Yes, isn't that amazing? Your (church) small group gifted that to you." Could there be a more perfect representation of Chance, of our situation? I think not. Because even though our son was gone, sweet life still had space to grow.

Death doesn't kill our spirits because through Jesus, we are given the opportunity to mature and press on and keep blooming and blessing the world with our fruit. Fruit that comes from our darkest moments is fruit that needs to be shared. Because even in death, beauty can shine and feed the world with its truth if we let it.

This tree now sits outside our sunroom window. I love its placement because it catches my eye several times a day. It's a Chinese fringe tree and blooms every April, the month of Chance's birth. Our friends are pretty amazing, no? I watch as tiny birds land on the tree and whistle out their song, and I am awed by the semblance and the faithfulness of my God. A God who is big and mighty and lavishes us with faithfulness and refuge and shields us with His truth. A God who reminds us that He is our true relief from life's desert walks.

"He will cover you with his feathers, and under his wings you will find refuge; his faithfulness will be your shield and rampart" (Psalm 91:4).

People joined voices in song as the service began, and my eyes drifted slightly ahead and to the right as several friends were running a bit behind and just making their way up to our gathering. I didn't know it at the time, but a train had stopped quite a few folks from making the 10:00 a.m. start. But this train? God blessed us with this train, this delay, because what it did was cause a purposeful and powerful visual for our family that can still bring me to tears. As "Lord, I Need You" was being strung on the guitar, a sea of blue balloons filled the air and flooded my sight. Family after family that had been hung up by that train came walking toward the pavilion, balloons in hand, and this visual was the perfect comfort in the perfect moment from our perfect God. Sometimes delays are just part of His plan.

Our minister, Mr. Ronnie, led the service and, oh, what a beautiful job he did. Countless people have commented to me that his words were so powerful and true and enlightening, that they were able to look at their own losses, look at death, through a completely new lens. With Mr. Ronnie's permission, a few points from his message.

"Chance Blackburn was created to glorify God. God's designs for Chance were decided before he was born. He would exist for the glory of God. Twenty weeks and three days of that work was on the earth. The rest will be in heaven. His conscious life—who he is fully intended to be, his obedience to his Maker—was appointed to be lived out in heaven. That is a good place to live for the glory of God! Woe to us if we think that the only place to glorify God is on this tiny planet! Chance was created to glorify God. He did, and he is. The purpose of Chance Michael Blackburn's life is to glorify God. And by God's either intentional or permissive will, Chance is purposed to begin his eternal service now. He took a shortcut and bypassed his time here.

"Chance Blackburn is happier today than the happiest person on earth has ever been. That he missed earth's pleasures of Little League and marriage and children and food and friends do not cause him the slightest regret. He took a shortcut to the life that is truly life. He took a much shorter route to the One in whose presence is fullness of joy and at whose right hand are pleasures for evermore. By comparison, the pleasures that Chance enjoys today make all of ours boring to the extreme. I wish he were here. He's in good hands now, but I wish he were here."

At the conclusion of his message, we, as one body, walked from under the pavilion to the open sky and, at the conclusion of a prayer, released our blue balloons up to the heavens. We watched them fly. We watched until the last balloon was out of sight. We watched in honor of Chance, in remembrance of him. We watched as a reminder that this world is not, in fact, our home, even though it can so easily feel like it. It was a reminder of hope and beauty and the joyful promise of eternity, where there will be no more pain or tears or ultrasounds gone bad. We like to say that the balloons made it to the pearly gates just in time for Chance's "Welcome to Heaven" party. I will never again look at a blue balloon quite the same.

Chapter 13

A Few Things about Grief

I t was a Friday night, exactly thirteen days since Chance's funeral. I was home alone with the girls while Brandon was at a baseball game with friends. This was the first night since we'd lost Chance that I would be alone for a significant amount of time. Being alone is not something that has ever bothered me, and quite frankly, I enjoy moments to myself, but during that time, as I was grieving the loss of my son, I craved faces and people and bodies.

I knew I was taking a risk. I was putting myself in a vulnerable situation, but kept telling myself it would be good for me and all would be okay. I also knew that Brandon needed some time out of the house, time with the boys, since that, in and of itself, was healing for him.

I got the girls in bed at the early hour of 6:30 p.m., ate a quick dinner (even though I still didn't feel like eating), and decided I would write some thank you notes, read a few blogs, and relax in bed for a little while.

And then the storm hit. I kid you not. Not just a little-bit-of-rain storm, but a storm so large I was scrambling for flashlights (and batteries because apparently we don't think to keep working batteries in flashlights) and candles. I huddled in the middle of my bed with my phone and my (working) flashlight and no electricity. The storm kept raging. Flashes of lightning lit up the sky outside my window. Thunder pounded, over and over and over. And the rain just kept coming down.

Because, of course. It was the first night that I was alone. In that moment, I let loose the tears that were inevitable. Home alone, storm raging both outside my window and inside my heart, and tears flowing because, goodness, I just wanted to hold my son again. I wanted to kiss his nose and stroke his little hat and stare at his precious face. But I couldn't.

Yet in that moment of deep vulnerability, I felt the Lord wrapping me up tightly, taking hold, and reminding me that, while right now life feels scary and sad and overwhelming, it is only time before the storm will cease and the sun will shine again. Because it will. God has proven this time and time again in my life and in yours. God promises we will not pass through this life without seasons of darkness. God also promises the dawn after the dark—every time. Light always wins.

Darkness has its hours, but light always wins.

So I lay there, with flashlight and phone, thunder and lightning, and I let myself cry, and I let myself smile, because God was and is still faithful. And regardless of my longing, even in my longing, His promises remain true, and His ways so very good.

The months following Chance's death were some of the hardest and darkest of my life. They were months where I felt numb to the world, alone in my sadness, bitter toward God's gifts to others, and confusion because, *really, God, do we need another ministry ... another page tab for my blog?* My physical body healed within weeks, yet my mind struggled to grasp our new reality. I had never experienced true, soul-stretching grief until we lost Chance. And I can now say that grief is a very real and very strange phenomenon.

Grief will come and go in epic waves, with many possible side effects—deep sadness, a depression-like state, anxiety, inability to make even the simplest of decisions, loneliness and the urge to isolate, inability to focus properly, preoccupation with death and dying, vivid dreams, insomnia. The five stages of grief are a real thing. Yet you won't necessarily work through them in set order; I didn't, anyway.

As you ride the waves of grief, just do the next thing. Just keep putting one foot in front of the other and do the next thing right in front of you. Don't think long-term. Think of the next few minutes. Eat that sandwich. Unload the dishwasher. Take your living children to the park. Take a shower. Just do the next thing, and eventually things will start to feel normal again.

People will make hurtful comments in the name of faith, yet these do typically come from a place of love and concern. Comments such as, "It was for the best," or, "At least you have your two girls," or "Don't be sad; he's in a better place," sting to the core. But people just don't know what to say, and at least people are saying *something*, because the hardest, most saddening part is when people don't say anything. By not saying anything, the experience and loss feel small and insignificant. But please, try to give people grace. They, like you, are doing their best.

People want to help, so tell people what you need. Tell people it brings you joy when you hear them speak your child's name. Tell people your spouse is working late or gone for business, and you just can't bear to be alone when night falls. Tell people you need to eat but have zero energy for preparing a meal. People will show up.

You never get over the loss of a child or ever fully move on, yet the grief becomes more manageable and happiness eventually outweighs sadness. You learn to live with your loss.

You will never be the same, yet through God's great mercies and the army of people surrounding you, you will heal and rebuild. You will eventually claim your tambourine and find your song once again.

A level of guilt comes once the happiness creeps back in. Please embrace the happiness and resist pushing it away. Cling to it with all your might. This is what our Father, and your child, wants for you.

Heaven will become so real and big, and this earth and all of its silly importance will fade. After Chance's passing, my frequent prayer was, *Jesus, please come today.* I meant it, and still do. No longer is one foot planted in heaven and the other on earth. Both feet are now planted in my heavenly home. I crave nothing more than eternity with Jesus. Knowing you have a child already there changes things. It puts life into proper perspective. This earthly home is just a gap, a phase between something good and something remarkably better.

The community of people you call friends and family will surprise you. People will walk alongside you, carrying you when your legs don't have the strength. People will organize food and send cards and texts and show up in so many unexpected ways. People will come out of the woodwork, showing their love and support while shouting the common thread of, "Together we are going to get through this."

Just as your people surprise you, so will your Heavenly Father. He is bigger than your grief, and He hurts and cries with you. He hears you. He is holding you in the palm of His hand and covering you with His feathers (Psalm 91). Loss can cause a griever to feel as though they have been abandoned, but abandonment is not in God's job description. He will gently remind you that grief has no timeline and tears are not a lack of faith, just a sign of tremendous love. His ways might not be our ways, yet He is faithful to pull us through to dry ground. Though we feel that our valley could get no lower, if we stay the course in trust and praise, He will lead our thirsty lips to fresh water.

He will not let you sink even on the worst of days. He is rooting for you. He is your rock when you feel you have no way to stand. You will be stretched and tested in new ways, but you will emerge stronger. You will emerge victorious. Hold on to His hope, dear sister. There is so much to be found.

"My soul finds rest in God alone; my salvation comes from him. He alone is my rock and my salvation, he is my fortress, I will never be shaken" (Psalm 62:1–2).

The concept of light versus darkness and letting light win was a main focus of my grief and eventual healing. Like the night of the storm, God continued to give me images of victorious light emerging from deep darkness. One image was of a sunrise. What I love about a sunrise is that it is a guarantee. The sun will always rise, regardless of your location, regardless of whether you are wandering the dry desert or skipping atop a flourishing mountain.

There is something about watching the sunrise each morning that captures my heart and, some mornings, takes my breath away. Especially since losing Chance. There is something so powerful about going to bed at night, darkness all around, yet awakening at that beautiful moment, that beautiful peek between dark and light. The dark is still there, still present, yet the light is visibly there too, touching the dark. It's that moment when dark and light intersect, and you know that, in a moment's time, the light will overcome. Because it always does. Day after day after day, no matter how dark the night, the light eventually breaks forth and wins.

In ways, it feels like yesterday that I was holding him, and in other ways, it feels like much more time has passed. I think about this phenomenon. How 365 days can feel like 365 seconds and also 365 years. How the darkness and the light of the last year and a half have been weaving together this amazingly ornate picture of tears, growth, longing, stretching, and beauty from ashes.

Beauty really can come from ashes if you let it.

Because no matter how dark the darkness feels, there is always the promise of pure light on the other side. Because the One who holds us in all our joy also holds us in all our sadness. Because if we just keep putting one foot in front of the other, even when we don't feel like it, even when our bodies want to resist, and keep searching endlessly for the sunrise, we will be so pleasantly surprised when we find it and realize that the light is winning and joy is already stirring.

"Then your light will break forth like the dawn, and your healing will quickly appear; then your righteousness will go before you, and the glory of the Lord will be your guard" (Isaiah 58:8).

Keep searching, friends. Keep striving for the light. Keep striving for the light that *does not burn out*. For the light always shines in the darkness and won't let the darkness claim victory (John 1:5). Keep searching for the beauty that comes from the ashes of your story. Choose to let God's gift of a sunrise sink deep and inspire you.

Choose to rise and shine.

The Reality of Our Tears

A huge misconception of grief is that tear-stained eyes equal a lack of faith. That if only we could muster a little more belief, then we could dry our eyes more quickly and move on. That our sadness somehow reveals our inability to trust His plans. This could not be further from the truth.

Several months after losing Chance, I received an e-mail devotional written by Max Lucado, produced by Faith Gateway. Max's words hit so very close to home. Max writes:

"Flooded eyes don't represent a faithless heart. A person can enter a cemetery Jesus-certain of life after death and still have a Twin Tower crater in the heart. Christ did. He wept, and he knew he was ten minutes from seeing a living Lazarus!

"And His tears give you permission to shed your own. Grief does not mean you don't trust; it simply means you can't stand the thought of another day without the Jacob or Lazarus of your life.

"If Jesus gave the love, He understands the tears. So grieve, but don't grieve like those who don't know the rest of this story." (FaithGateway.com 2015)

As I sat reading, the tears started to come. I cried for the first time in a good while because it was as if God was using Max to say,

"It's okay. Your tears don't mean you don't trust my ways. Your tears don't mean your faith is any less valid. Your longing for your son is normal. Your tears have meaning, so let them fall. Don't hold back. Just let them fall."

My tears should not produce feelings of guilt or shame or embarrassment because, while I claim Jesus's path for me as perfect, I am a mommy who misses her only son. I miss my son more than words can express. I am a mommy who is sad because the son I held in my arms is no longer here for the embracing.

I was encouraged because, as Max points out, I know how the story ends. I know the secret to this whole messy thing of a life. I know that ultimately Christ died—paid the ultimate price, the ultimate suffering—and moved mountains while on this earth so that we can stand firm on hope, even in the midst of the tears, in midst of our desert wandering.

We grieve, but we know the rest of the story. I can't imagine not. Can you? So I have to share it. Because somewhere, someone is sitting hopeless and hurting and thinking their Lazarus is gone and that is it, the end of the story—the grave won the final tug between life and death. But a sweeter day is coming, friends. A day when the tears stop for good and all the ones who have gone before will greet us and show us around and proclaim how much sweeter heaven is than anything they ever experienced on earth.

Let's grieve and cry and let ourselves go there, but let's remember the rest of the story. Because the rest of the story has the final word. Hope wins. Joy abounds.

> I pray also that the eyes of your heart may be enlightened in order that you may know the hope to which he has called you, the riches of his glorious inheritance in the saints, and his incomparable great power for us who believe. That power is like the working of his mighty strength, which he exerted in Christ when he raised him from the dead and

seated him at his right hand in the heavenly realms. (Ephesians 1:18–20)

Where Pain and Peace Collide

I think there comes a point after any loss, trauma, or life-altering event when both pain and peace take up residence in your heart. When sadness is still a very real emotion, yet deep down, there is peace and contentment. When grief and sorrow still bring you to your knees, yet deep down, there is comfort and hope—opposite emotions living in one space. In one moment, tears are shed, and in the next, tears are replaced by an overwhelming sense of joy. Your heart literally aches while at the same time it feels settled and calm.

I had constant longing for my son that translated into a constant longing for Jesus. This was and is my reality. It will always be my reality. Pain and peace can dance together as we journey through our unique desert places.

Peace. It does not mean to be in a place with no noise, trouble, or hard work. It means to be in the midst of those things and still be calm in your heart.—Author Unknown

I read somewhere the idea that faith doesn't necessarily make our situations any less painful, but faith keeps us from being swallowed or overtaken by our pain. I have to agree. There has not been one day since losing Chance where the pain hasn't shown up. Yet even in the midst of my hurt, God has given me an underlying sense of calm and overwhelming peace. I felt it the second I looked into my son's face, a moment I will never forget. I am so thankful for this balance with which God is gracing me. The daily tears are no longer there, the daily breaking down in sobs has ceased, but my mind still thinks of my son daily. God continues to remind me that He is strong enough and big enough and loving enough to keep moving me forward in faith and trust. And in that moving forward, as faith builds and trust grows, a deeper beauty is, in time, revealed.

Don't Worry; You Won't Remind Me of My Loss

Since losing our son, friends and readers have come to me, sharing that their friend or family member has also experienced such a loss. They have the burning desire to reach out, but don't know exactly how to go about doing so without scraping an already open wound. "How can I help? What is the best thing for me to do without causing additional sadness? I really want to check in, but I don't want to make them cry, so I have just been giving them some space. I have been praying, but I'm hesitant to ask because I am worried I will awaken their pain."

I understand this way of thinking. I used to think this same way before holding Chance in my arms, studying his face so intently because the moments with him were few. I used to keep grieving mommas and wives and families at a distance *because, goodness, I don't want to be the cause of any more grief.* I surely do not want to be responsible for more heartache.

But, dear friend of a friend who just experienced a traumatic loss, let me be clear, as one walking on the other side. Please don't hesitate to ask. Please don't hesitate when you feel the urge to call or text or seek out that loss mom or dad in person. Please don't hesitate to say their child's name out loud. Hearing their child's name is music to their ears. Beautiful heavenly music. It is refreshing and reassuring knowing that, while our children aren't living on this earth, they are living on in the minds and hearts of those around us. And while I understand that you are concerned your words might cause tears to swell, please don't worry …

You won't remind me of my loss.

My loss is a part of my every day, just as my living husband and children are a part of my every day. Loss becomes a puzzle piece of our new, everyday normal. There has not been one day since April

4, 2015 where my thoughts have not turned to my little guy. He is on my mind all the time. When I think of my girls, I think of my son. That is just how it works now.

You won't remind me of my loss.

Because I never forget.

So while you might think twice about stopping that hurting momma at the grocery store or seeking her out after Sunday school or sending her that Facebook message when she crosses your mind, let these words give you permission to stop and seek out. Your words won't bring more tears or more hurt or more grief. I promise you they won't. In fact, your words bring the opposite.

Your words bring *hope.*

Your words bring *life.*

Your words bring *peace.*

Your words bring *joy,* even if accompanied by a few tears.

Because we never forget.

Redeeming Suffering

Several weeks after Chance's funeral, a sweet friend from church stopped me when she spotted me across the church aisle. "I want you to know I have been praying for you. Specifically, I have been praying that God would reveal to you the purpose in Chance's life." With that one simple sentence, her prayer became my prayer too. I had never thought to pray this prayer, but in that moment, it sounded so profound. And it sure sounded like a good way to turn this tragedy back to truth.

So I would pray day after day after day, "God, please reveal to me the unique purpose in Chance's short life. Show me. Make it known the purpose in what currently feels like constant pain. Give some meaning to this, Father."

I was overwhelmed and some days overtaken by the reality of our experience, and I learned quickly that amidst all my racing thoughts, I also had to ask the Father to clear my mind, my head, in order to make space for His answer. This was key in my ability to listen.

Sarah Young writes in *Jesus Today,* "Your racing thoughts make it hard to hear My gentle whisper" (2012). She pairs this thought with a powerful verse in 1 Kings: "After the earthquake came a fire, but the Lord was not in the fire. And after the fire came a gentle whisper" (1 Kings 19:12).

My earthquake had come. The fire had blazed. But, in that moment, the day my friend stopped me at church, I was sitting in that space, the aftermath of the storm, where I could choose to focus on the gentle whispers of the Father. I kept praying and searching and asking and listening. And over time, I heard His reply.

"Jesus."

The purpose in Chance's short life and stillbirth and burial is the sweet reminder of the promise of Jesus. The promise of heaven. The promise that there is so much more to life than the day-to-day grind that so easily bogs down my heart and my head. There is so much more than what I see with my eyes. "When you think of Chance, may you always think of Me. When the world hears of Chance, may they always be reminded of Me." Such a tender answer from a tender God.

Although I don't believe God wanted Chance to die, I do believe He allowed it to happen for His good and His glory. His greater purposes. For the pointing back to His Son.

And while this belief does not remove suffering or instantly heal the hurt, it does redeem it.

My prayer for those reading this, for those of you going through your own personal earthquake or blazing fire or wilderness journey, is that you can find purpose in the pain. That you can clear your mind and still your heart to hear the Lord's sweet, gentle whispers. That you can look at your circumstance through eyes focused on the cross. And that the Lord will grant grace and peace by redeeming your suffering and covering it with meaning.

So to our Father, we join hands and say, *"Enter our hurts, Lord.*

Redeem each and every one. Breathe fresh perspective into our hearts that are aching today. Instill hope where there is none. Permeate the calloused areas. Give us Your gentle whispers. Break down walls erected out of pride or bitterness or anger or utter sadness and despair. Show us purpose. Point us to Jesus.

"Redeem our suffering."

Real Talk: What circumstance has you pleading with God to redeem your suffering and to help you see purpose in the pain?

Action Steps: Whatever your hurt, whatever cross you are carrying today, lay it down at His feet and ask boldly, in His name, that He replace despair with hope and clouded vision with fresh eyes to see His handiwork.

From the Mouth of Babes

We could probably agree that children say the funniest things. I love reading blog or Facebook posts from parents documenting the hilarious thoughts coming from the minds and mouths of their children.

Yet along with the hilarious, children also say the sweetest, dearest things. They are so much wiser than we give them credit for, and their minds are always thinking, remembering, and even drawing hope from tragedy. Over the past year, several friends have shared conversations they have had with their children about our son, Chance, and how he is now in heaven. These stories, these conversations, bring us so much joy and indescribable hope, friends. Please don't ever stop sharing them with Brandon and me. Please don't ever stop sharing them with the loss momma and daddy in your own life. These stories from the mouths of your children continue to help us process as we make our way through the crazy realities of grief.

Six months after Chance's funeral, as I was hopping in the car to take Clara to school, I received the following text from my longtime childhood friend, Emily. She described a conversation she had the night before with her son, Conner.

Emily: *"I would call you … but I can't without crying. So I'm sorry! But I wanted you to know that last night when we were praying, Conner started crying after. Like major. He said he was scared to go to heaven without anyone he knew. All of a sudden he says, 'Wait!! We will know someone in heaven! We will know Riley and your friend's baby boy!' He then recounted every detail of the service for Chance. Thank you for sharing that day with us."*

Me: *"Oh my goodness! That is the best. It's stories like this that bring me such joy and peace and hope!! So thank you for sharing. Squeeze Conner for me."*

Several weeks after Chance's funeral, my friend Lindsey texted me with the most beautiful picture that her daughter, Ava, painted as she processed the service. Ava led the prayer at their dinner table that particular evening, and after her usual words, she said this: "And, God, we don't know why Ms. Brittnie's baby had to die. Please help us. We are sad."

Oh, to have faith like a child.

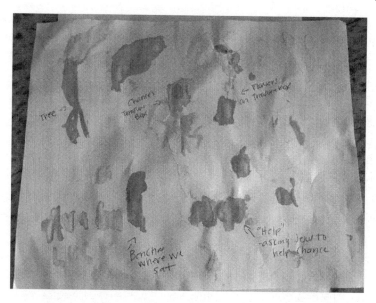

There are so many other stories I could share. Stories of babes surprising us with flowers and a heartfelt note on Chance's grave the day of his due date because they knew we would make a visit. Stories of children processing death while also gaining the understanding that, while death is sad and seems scary, they do not have to fear. They do not have to fear because they now know a child that went on to heaven before them.

God is using our son to make heaven real and big and beautiful in the minds of little babes.

If this isn't beauty from ashes, beauty arising from my darkest desert place, I'm not sure what is.

Just Show Up

My biggest piece of advice for those walking alongside a family member or friend who is experiencing loss, or who is spending time in their own desert land, is to just show up. Just show up. No fancy words needed. No explanations or reasoning required. Just your body, just your presence. Maybe a hug and an "I'm so sorry; this is so awful." A "Together we will get through this" won't hurt either. There is power in presence. Hope rises when we stand as one.

There is a beautiful picture of people showing up in Exodus 17. The Israelites were being attacked by the Amalekites, so Moses and Joshua kicked it into gear and formulated a plan. Joshua would lead the men to battle, and Moses would stand steady at the top of the hill with God's staff firm in his hands. As the battle began, Moses held the staff up above his head, toward the heavens. As long as he did this, the Israelites were coming in ahead, but as soon as he grew weary and his hands began to fall, the Amalekites would make a comeback. When Moses's hands began to falter, his people showed up for relief.

> So Joshua fought the Amalekites as Moses had ordered, and Moses, Aaron and Hur went to the top of the hill. As long as Moses held up his hands, the Israelites were winning, but whenever he lowered his hands, the Amalekites were winning. *When Moses' hands grew tired, they took a stone and put it under him and he sat on it. Aaron and Hur held his hands up—one on one side, one on the other—so that his hands remained steady till sunset.* (Exodus 17:10–12, emphasis added)

In case you don't know how the battle ends ... the Israelites win.

When we lost Chance, our people showed up, and they showed up in *big* ways. Crisis called, and our community answered. Meals, desserts, breakfasts, childcare, their prayers, their time, their financial resources, tangible gifts to help preserve Chance's memory—all of these things were offered, no strings attached. What a gift! What a blessing! I am so thankful for all of these people, each and every one. You know who you are. Thank you for your love, your care, and for showing up. You were Jesus in the flesh. You were our Aaron and Hur. Beauty poured through your words and your actions. Your kindness will never be forgotten and will forever serve as a reminder of how to give big and love well.

Chapter 14

Choosing Joy

I wish there were some easy answer. Some easy formula for defaulting to joy when life gets hard and messy and ugly. Some easy way to tie this all up with a pretty bow. That would be too easy, I suppose. At times, it seems simple to choose joy, like when you know your hardship will only last a season. But sometimes our desert walks last beyond a season or two, possibly forever. That's when choosing joy gets a little trickier—when you realize you are in this for the long haul and your choice is either to choose joy or to crumble in the name of disappointment and eventually die under that name.

But the good news is that Jesus gives us the choice. It's by keeping our eyes on Him and not our circumstances that we have the space and perspective to choose hope and joy and everlasting contentment. This choice is what allows us to take up our tambourines in praise, whether or not God chooses to deliver us from the desert. We can choose to praise regardless.

Because at the end of the day, it's about Jesus, not my circumstances.

That moment I realized my weight loss was completely out of control? That moment I got the call from genetics? That moment I received my oldest child's diagnosis? That moment the technician told me my baby was gone? It is my reaction to these moments that make or break me, that make or break you too.

We can choose to let Satan enter our hearts and slowly sink all the faith, hope, and peace we know to be true, or we can choose joy. *Joy.* Joy in the midst of confusion. Joy in the midst of this new roller coaster of emotions that could take me straight down to the depths of despair or straight up to a constant source of life and hope.

"You have made known to me the path of life; you will fill me with joy in your presence" *(*Psalm 16:11).

Choosing joy doesn't mean the path will instantly be easy or all of life's hardships will be immediately relieved. The last few years have been filled with some very hard moments for us as a family. Very hard moments, on many levels, mixed with lots of searching and begging of God and unanswered prayers. Sometimes joy seems counterintuitive.

But true joy is found when we step out in trust, regardless of how many prayers have been answered.

In *Choose JOY* by Sara Frankl and Mary Carver, Frankl states:

> When people say they can't see the good coming from the pain, my answer is that it's not our job to know. It's God's. It's just our job to trust, whether we see it or not, that He brings beauty from the ashes. And maybe the beauty won't show up in my life. Maybe it will bring beauty to someone I'll never meet. My job is simply to trust Him. To go through the physical and emotional pain and embrace the peace of knowing that He is taking care of it. It's not about how bad the pain is. It's about how good our God is (2016).

Choosing joy stems from the deep belief that everything God brings into my life is good. Let that sit for a moment. That can be hard to swallow. Is a scale that reads eighty-nine pounds and a fight for life a gift? Is shooting yourself with needles and taking endless amounts of hormones to conceive praiseworthy? Is a child's intellectual disability truly a good thing? Is a baby dying in the womb good news? On the surface, no, but if I believe that God's ways are perfect and His plans sovereign, then I have to accept that whatever He brings my way is good. Even if that good is tearing my heart wide open.

Several chapters later, Frankl goes on to state:

> I don't know if I'm right or wrong, but I trust that everything that comes from God is good. I trust that everything that comes from God is an already answered prayer. I trust that everything that will come from God is exactly what I need. Even if it's hard. Because He sees what I can't. So I count it all a gift. And I thank Him—not for the pain and the difficulty—but for the faithfulness He gives during it all. That is how I have learned to praise. Even in my weakest places, even in my hardest moments, even in the depths of pain and sickness, I thank Him for what I know for sure is true—beyond the distraction of the hard, within the hard. I praise Him for Him (2016).

Recently, I have been reflecting on my early days of blogging. Those early days? They seem so very long ago. My little space on the internet was born in mid-2011, as a way to process the ups and downs of eating disorder recovery, and soon after, our desire to become pregnant with our first child. All I can say is wow, what a journey. What a roller coaster the last few years have been. So much joy and happiness, but so many questions and tears mixed in too.

Riding the extreme highs and lows hasn't been easy, but it has been worth it.

At the end of 2015, I read a devotional on Genesis, and the author presented on Abraham and how sometimes the greatest faith of all is our ability to trust God's processes to get to His promises. Oh, how true this is for me. We know God's ways are good and faithful and ultimately work for our best, yet it is often the seasons of waiting and watching that cause us to question God's intentions and plans. The waiting and watching cause us to ask, "God, did you *really* hear me? Are you *really* working for my good? Because I am still holding out for your Promised Land, and my mouth is dry and my feet are tired and I am just not sure how much longer I can walk this desert place."

"But as for me, I watch in hope for the Lord, I wait for God my Savior; my God will hear me" (Micah 7:7).

Getting to some of God's greatest promises requires a faith like Abraham or Moses's. Attaining those promises we desire sometimes requires a lot of crying out with eyes wide open, watching expectantly for God to move. And the hard part? Waiting. The wilderness wandering that starts as three weeks and morphs into forty years, or possibly a lifetime. Yet we do not wait in our own strength. In our own strength, we would surely choose to reside in the desert forever.

In those early days of recovering from an eating disorder, I cried. I waited. And God heard (Micah 7:7). In those early days of fertility treatments and all the shots and pills and blood draws and emotional turmoil, I cried. I waited. God heard (Micah 7:7). In those early days of mothering Clara, noticing something was amiss with both her physical and social development, I cried. I waited. God heard (Micah 7:7). In physically delivering a child who was then taken from my arms to be buried in the ground, I cried. I waited. God heard (Micah 7:7).

I would be foolish to think there will be no more tears and no more seasons where God asks me to wait and watch. The tears and the wait change based on circumstance, but our God does not. He always sees. He always hears. He always invites us to trek the valley in hopes that we walk and wait with hope, through His processes, for His promises on the other side.

Let's ask that the scales be removed from our eyes so that, even when our feet stand on the sand, our lips thank Him. Let's see Him and not our desert places. Let's sleep in peace because we believe He is bigger than our mess. Let's choose the joy.

"You have *filled my heart with greater joy* than when their grain and new wine abound. *I will lie down and sleep in peace*, for *you alone, O Lord, make me dwell in safety*" (Psalm 4:7–8, emphasis added).

Turning Parched Ground into Springs

I stumbled upon Isaiah 41 one recent morning, and the words hit me in a new way, like never before. I love when God surprises me like that. Scriptures I have read time and time again suddenly jump off the page with fresh meaning and fresh hope. He knew I needed these words. This hope. This promise. This reminder to choose joy in all things.

> The poor and needy search for water, but there is none; their tongues are parched with thirst. *But I the Lord will answer them; I, the God of Israel, will not forsake them. I will make rivers flow on barren heights, and springs within the valleys. I will turn the desert into pools of water, and the parched ground into springs.* I will put in the desert the cedar and the acacia, the myrtle and the olive. I will set junipers in the wasteland, the fir and cypress together, so that people may see and know, may consider and understand, that the hand of the Lord has done this, that the Holy One of Israel has created it. (Isaiah 41:17–20)

So many times, I want to drink my own water. Hard times come, frustrating situations happen, death strikes, and I try to satisfy my thirst with my own agenda, my own sense of control. I am sure you have been there a time or two.

Yet what God is really saying here is *just be still.* Just wait with hope. Just hold on a second longer because while you are searching, *I am fighting for you.*

So many times, I am so preoccupied with my own thirst that I miss the bigger picture, just like the Israelites. I know that God is trustworthy and His ways best, yet when hardships come, I am quick to grumble. I miss the joy pool of water right in front of me. The overflowing spring right in front of my big brown eyes.

Are you searching for water? Overwhelmed with what feels like an unquenchable thirst? Smack in the middle of your own personal desert, whatever that may be? Just keep holding on, friends, because God is fighting.

God is using you and your story to move mountains.

That dry, brittle ground you now see will soon transform into a beautiful wellspring of life. That's the promise. Your joy pool is for the taking.

He Remains

Wilderness wandering, working through our grief, and various life disappointments can certainly take more time than we expect. The Israelites wandered and waited for relief for forty years in the desert—forty years! That many years, friends. But it is when we are faithful in these desert places, laying down our expectations of this life as an act of trust and replacing these expectations with a joyful attitude, accepting whatever comes our way as best, that we are able to take up our tambourines once and for all—regardless of how many years we have left in the desert. We must remember that God is in our corner, working wonders. He raises the bar, calls us to the desert to reveal His power and might and intricate miracles, and to remind us that through it all, *He remains.* He is constant so that, in all of our hurts, we constantly point the world back to Him.

"But I have raised you up for this very purpose, that I might show you my power and that my name might be proclaimed in all the earth" (Exodus 9:16).

We can smile in the desert; we can choose joy. Because He remains through the sad and happy and laughter and the unable-to-function moments. He is the same yesterday, today, and forever. Forever. Chance can attest to that, my friends.

The morning of Chance's due date, I woke and asked the Lord, "Give me a fresh word today. Please give me something new to hold onto as I go into this weekend of my son's should-have-been birthday. Reveal yourself to me so this weekend will be filled with much celebration, despite the circumstance." And He gave me Psalm 102.

> In the beginning you laid the foundations of the earth, and the heavens are the work of your hands. *They will perish, but you remain;* they will all wear out like a garment. Like clothing you will change them and they will be discarded. *But you remain the same, and your years will never end.* (Psalm 102:25–27).

The cradle might be empty, but our hearts are not.

Because He remains.

God Is Working in This Season

I have always loved the idea of a season changing. Pulling out new clothes that have been stored (well, depending on where you live, I suppose), gearing up for new foods and new smells (the best thing about fall is pumpkin everything, no?), and a clean slate for a fresh start in areas that might need a little attention. I am reminded of the well-quoted section of scripture in Ecclesiastes 3.

For everything there is a season, and a time for every matter under heaven:

> a time to be born, and a time to die;
> a time to plant, and a time to pluck up what is planted;
> a time to kill, and a time to heal;
> a time to break down, and a time to build up;
> a time to weep, and a time to laugh;
> a time to mourn, and a time to dance;
> a time to cast away stones, and a time to gather stones together;
> a time to embrace, and a time to refrain from embracing;
> a time to seek, and a time to lose;
> a time to keep, and a time to cast away;
> a time to tear, and a time to sew;
> a time to keep silent, and a time to speak;
> a time to love, and a time to hate;
> a time for war, and a time for peace ...

> He has made everything beautiful in its time. He has set eternity in the hearts of men; yet they cannot fathom what God has done from the beginning to the end. I know that there is nothing better for men than to be happy and do good while they live. That everyone may eat and drink, and find satisfaction in *ALL* his toil—this is a gift of God." (Ecclesiastes 3:1–8, 11–13)

Oh, how these verses bring me joy and hope. God is telling us here that yes, we will all have trouble and sadness and heartbreak and war, but He makes all things new. All things. Not just some of them or ones He deems worthy of renewal, but *all* of them.

He takes that season of waiting and weeping and turns it into the biggest dance party we have ever seen. He takes that season of loneliness and questioning and turns it into community and security. He takes that season of pruning and plucking and turns it into *an abundance of fruit*. There is so much promise hidden inside Ecclesiastes 3.

Whatever season you find yourself in today, may I encourage you to find hope in His promises? Take heart because the season will indeed change. Maybe not in your timeframe or in the way you envision, but it will indeed change. For every season you find yourself in, there is the promise of a new day and a new start, and, possibly, a new perspective. God is working so hard behind the scenes that we cannot remotely fathom the goodness in store.

God is always working behind the scenes for our good.

When we truly believe this, and I mean truly believe it, that makes choosing joy an easier option. If I believe He is at constant work for my best, then my reaction of thanks and praise and joy naturally flows. It becomes automatic because I want His best for me. Don't you? Even if His best is having me walk the desert for a while longer, for a lifetime, that is what I want. I don't want to settle for a mediocre blueprint. I don't want to trade God's best for whatever good I am able to conjure up in my mind and with my eyes, because my eyes are so limited when it comes to God's big picture. I want His best! I don't want to miss the fruit of His ways! And sometimes His best looks like a child with limited abilities or a casket fit for a baby doll.

Sometimes God's best gifts can only be revealed by walking the desert with Him.

Let's meditate on this good news. That our mourning will in fact turn to dancing. That the light will impede the darkness and is guaranteed to win. That the trees won't remain barren forever. That the leaves will come, and colors will shine, and joy will abound. That this season you are facing today can change—we just have to change the focus of our hearts and the lenses on our glasses.

In changing the lenses, we are not negating the facts. The desert is real and dark and scary and intimidating and fear-inducing and filled with sadness and hurts and lost dreams and head-hanging and tears shed and lots and lots of questions. Sometimes the desert makes us want to run and hide forever, maybe even give up. There are emotions so high and grief so intense, you don't know how you will make it one more day.

Choosing joy is an act of trust, and it could be the difference between life or death, physically, emotionally, or spiritually. Choosing joy does not negate the hurt, the hard stuff. But if we lift our head, just a little bit, we can see the rainbow that remains once the storm begins to clear. The intricate tapestry God has been weaving together since we first set foot in this dry land. The stretching and pruning and growth and healing is all so very, very beautiful.

This journey we are on in our own personal wastelands? Goodness, it's hard, isn't it? But let's not run away. Instead, let's run to Him. Let's keep our eyes open to Him and only on Him because then will we see loveliness begin to emerge. Let's look for His glory, His love song, even in our desert places.

Thank you, Jesus, for always working for our best, for gifting us with these desert walks, and for the promise to make all things new.

Let's keep putting one foot in front of the other, weary traveler. There's a song waiting to be sung.

Our tambourines await.

> This is what the Lord says: "The people who survive the sword will find favor in the desert; I will come to give rest to Israel." The Lord appeared to us in the past, saying: "I have loved you with an everlasting love; I have drawn you with loving kindness. I will build you up again and you will be rebuilt, O Virgin Israel. Again you will take up your tambourines." (Jeremiah 31:2–4)

Works Cited

Chapter 1:

- Dictionary.com. 2016. "Comparison." Last modified December 12. http://www.dictionary.com/browse/comparison?s=t
- Dictionary.com. 2016. "Control." Last modified December 12. http://www.dictionary.com/browse/control?s=t

Chapter 2:

- First5.org. 2016. "More Moments About Exodus 7." Last modified Jan 12. http://first5.org/plans/Exodus/ff_exodus_7

Chapter 3

- Weather.gov. 2016. "Hurricane Ike Synopsis." Last modified Dec 12. http://www.weather.gov/lix/ike_synopsis

Chapter 5:

- First5.org. 2016. "The Best Place To Look." Last modified Dec 12. http://first5.org/plans/Exodus/ff_exodus_16

Chapter 7:

- Ivfconnections.com. 2010. "Eating Disorders, Infertility and Pregnancy." Last modified Dec 12.

http://www.ivfconnections.com/forums/content.
php/205-Eating-Disorders-Infertility-and-Pregnancy

Chapter 8:

- Eugene Peterson. The Message: The Bible In Contemporary Language. (Colorado Springs: NavPress Publishing Group, 2002), 1599.
- Joan Ryan. The Water Giver: The Story of a Mother, a Son, and Their Second Chance. (New York: Simon and Schuster, 2009), page number unknown.

Chapter 13:

- FaithGateway.com. 2015. by Max Lucado 2015. "Jesus Weeps." Last modified Dec 12. http://www.faithgateway. com/grieving-charleston-sc-jesus-weeps/#.WE8DRjvqfES
- Sarah Young. Jesus Today. (Nashville: Thomas Nelson, 2012), 96.

Chapter 14:

- Sara Frankl and Mary Carver. Choose Joy. (New York: Faith Words Hachette Book Group, 2016), 31, 110.

Acknowledgments

Thank you to each and every one of you who played a role in this journey. I am beyond grateful that you believed in me, supported me, and encouraged me to follow God's leading.

Thank you to my husband, Brandon, who never once doubted this calling and who always responded to my insecurities with, "If God told you to write a book, well, then write it." Brandon, you have stood by my side for the last nine years, through all of these trials and joys, and I praise God that He gifted you to me. I cannot imagine doing life with anyone else. When the road gets rocky, you never lose hope and never lose faith. You lead our family exceptionally well, and I am honored to be your wife. I love you.

Thank you to my parents, who raised me to love the Lord and to seek Him first. Thank you for your example of faith through the desert, and for always pointing me back to Jesus when life feels hard. Thank you for teaching me the importance of prayer and the power that arises when we ask God to lead us into His will.

Ashley, Susan, and James, y'all are amazing, and I couldn't have handpicked better siblings. I love and appreciate each of you and the ways you have supported me over the years. Some of my most fun memories are with you. I think back on how God handcrafted our family, and while loss is never wished for, it is evident God had His hand in each of our stories. I debated including a picture of us from childhood, but I refrained. Oh, and thank you for not laughing at me when I mentioned I felt called to write a book. I love y'all!

A huge thank you to my friend Kelly, who told me approximately five hundred times, "You know, you really should write a book." Thank you for never giving up on me and listening to God when He asked you to reach out to me those many years ago. Your deep love and bold faith are a witness for Jesus and the gospel message.

To my First Family and A.C.U. people, thank you for always believing in me and showing up to hold my hand when life gets messy. Y'all have walked into the desert with me, more than once, when you could have easily just walked the perimeter. I am forever grateful. Thank you for being purposeful with your love, your wisdom, and your hope.

Thank you to the blogging community for your acceptance and friendship. It is amazing how true friends can be formed across miles and computer screens. While I have only met a handful of you in person, you have each played a role in the creation of this book ... your comments, your jokes, your encouragement, and your faith. Never stop writing.

Julie Parker, I hope you know how much I appreciate your time and your gift of editing. Thank you for taking on this project. And thank you, from the bottom of my (redundant) heart, for deleting one thousand unnecessary words from this manuscript. You're the best!

Thank you to WestBow Press, for believing in this message and taking a chance on a no-name writer like myself. It has been a privilege working with you!

And last, but certainly not least, a huge thank You to my Lord and Savior, Jesus Christ. Thank You for always leading me, always protecting me, and always working for my best. Thank You for Your wisdom and for Your tender, gentle whispers. Thank You for calling me perfect in Your eyes. Thank You for changing my life. And thank You for the promise of life after death, and that joy is always within reach.

Made in the USA
San Bernardino, CA
18 February 2017